I0141738

Barely Zen: A Completely Unscientific Guide To Life

Copyright © 2025 Steve Marsh

First Edition, Steve Marsh, Sunshine Coast, Australia

For permissions, inquiries, or additional resources, contact: contact@stemarsh.com

Introduction

Welcome to Barely Zen: A Completely Unscientific Guide To Life. A simple and yet effective way of approaching life and its challenges. Whilst I don't claim to be an expert, deep philosopher, scientist or guru. I believe my outlook and skills have allowed me to adapt and appreciate different areas of life. Some of the things I have discovered, things that I apply to my daily life I believe can help others in some way. Maybe you'll take a lot away, the fact that you are reading it is just an awesome start for me, perhaps you'll take a little bit away from it, and maybe you'll take nothing away. That's life. How did I get here? A few years ago I felt the urge to write, I wasn't 100% sure what it would be or what it would be about, but something that would take the learnings and thoughts out of my head and put them down on 'paper' to share with others. I've never written a book before and to be honest the thought hadn't really crossed my mind until a few years ago. A couple of instances in my life have created this inkling or urge, both instances were small incidents, but actually quite significant that they stayed with me. One was many years ago when I was with friends and I was rambling, as I often can, about different topics and my viewpoints. I wasn't being judgemental or trying to impact wisdom and knowledge just voicing my views and thoughts on a few different topics. I was and have never been any kind of ranter but I can waffle a lot in the correct company. I was chatting away and my friend mentioned, in passing, that I should write a book on all these thoughts. I'm pretty sure it was a throw away comment and he was 99% joking, but for some reason that statement stuck in my head for years. I did nothing with it, it would come and go and I would just let it go. Then many years later, I was chatting to another friend about my viewpoints and they randomly asked if I'd thought of doing a Ted talk. That thought had never crossed my mind (and I'm not sure I ever would a Ted talk), but deep down in my subconscious this statement along with the statement from many years ago seemed to merge together. Again I never did anything with it, but I did feel like these two very different and very separated statements were guiding me down a path. I did nothing and let it go again once more. However, and finally, circumstances led me to being on a train from York to Manchester in the UK on my own. I had a few hours to spare with nothing to do but stare out of the train window, the thought of writing had come and gone many times, but on that day I decided today was the day and here we are. I'm not sure how it will flow and It will likely bounce around from topic to topic but let's see how things pan out.

This book will flow with chapters on certain things, ways of thinking, habits that I believe allow me to make the most of life. Hopefully you can find these useful too or it will help you find your own words of wisdom. I'll also try to keep the chapters short, as I've found for me that's the best way to read. I don't like long chapters where the end never seems to be in sight. Short, direct and punchy is what I like and I hope it allows you to flow through this book, taking some or all of the information provided in this to help you with your daily life. Think of it as a manual to life you can easily dive in and out of. At the end of each chapter you'll find zenbites, a very quick summary of the chapter and zenquests, quick and simple tasks to allow you to put some of the things you've just read about into practice and get your mind moving. Throughout I'll reference mind / ego and soul / spirit. My definitions of these are that your mind is your ego, it's job is to look after you. It's the logical part of you when it comes to decisions and viewpoints. Your soul is your inner spirit and gut feeling, it's your deep down emotions and beliefs that aren't tarnished by the world around you. It's your true self. In a situation your mind may say this is the logical thing to do, let's do it and move forward, but your soul may be saying this doesn't feel right, pause and don't move forward. Your mind controls your body and your thoughts, taking its inputs from the world and outputting viewpoints and actions. Your soul is your inner compass and underlying beliefs. Sometimes they may contradict each other, my head says do this, but my heart says do that. If that ever happens, go with your heart. Your heart is the inner you, allow yourself to listen to it. Your soul, spirit, heart, or whatever word feels comfortable to you is your intuition coming through. We'll discuss this more later, let's get started.

I am not an expert, everything and anything written is my viewpoint and doesn't constitute medical advice. There are no specific scientific studies that resolve any of these topics, although there may be studies out there that corroborate my thoughts. Many of the topics look at things from a simple view, maybe too simple for those who have an analytical and deep thinking mind, but in my experience most things in life are simple and are easier to understand and importantly remember when they are simplified. These are my own opinions and views, some you may agree with, some you may not, hey you might not agree with any of them. This is your experience and it's down to your judgement how the topics resonate with you. If you are experiencing hard times please get in touch with your local doctor or helpline.

Now....let's get started.

MIND & BODY

Chapter 1: Stress

I open the book with what I think is one of the biggest impacts on people's lives. Stress. In all its forms stress can have a great impact on a person's life, it affects the mind and body in ways most cannot imagine or even know what is occurring. When people think of stress they often think of a busy work day, meeting deadlines, stressful meetings, planning a party, strained relationships. These are obvious stressful moments, they're big and they do affect your life in many ways but they are visible and conscious, you can feel and see them you know you are in the stressful moment. In these instances you may take time out or speak to someone, you may not. You are usually aware that these things are happening and sometimes you will give yourself a well earned rest afterward. Stress can also come in the form of what I call 'small' stressors. These are small stressful situations that you may not be conscious of, they are hidden and you are unaware they are even happening to you. They grind away in the background. An example of this is say you love chocolate (replace any small treat here), it's your treat in life, you adore it, crave it but stop yourself from having even the most tiny piece. This is a form of stress. It might not appear to fall into this category, but you are putting your mind through a level of anxiety that creates stress by not having what you desire. Sure, there is no benefit of eating all the chocolate you want, but at the same time depriving yourself of a simple treat creates stress within your mind and therefore your body. You create a level of anxiety within yourself as you are depriving yourself of something. That something could be huge or small, but the same principle applies, you are depriving yourself of something. This principle can be applied to many areas of life in which a small seemingly significant thing can create a level of stress within you. Kids are a great example, they don't get a small treat and they absolutely lose the plot over a small, seemingly significant thing, but to them the size of the treat doesn't matter, it's the fact that they have been deprived of the treat. The same applies to adults, no matter how big or small the 'treat' is, they are depriving themselves of something that their mind would like. Let's be honest sometimes this need will be unreasonable and with a little bit of time you think "I didn't need that, I was being annoying". However, other times you will be perfectly justified in your need. Another example is not giving yourself time to do something that you want to do, you create an excuse or reason to put it off. However, in your mind you are preventing your soul from following its will. Your soul wants to spend that extra 15 minutes in the shower, it wants to sit on the beach with no disturbances for an hour, but you say no to yourself, and you move on with your day without giving yourself that time. Did you move on? Maybe you did, but maybe you didn't. You prevented yourself from doing that small indulgence for yourself and therefore created a small amount of anxiety within yourself that creates a level of stress. Sure you can't spend all day in the shower, but you can spend that extra few minutes to reward yourself. You prevented yourself from giving yourself a little slice of joy. It's something you wanted to do, you didn't do it and it can create these little micro moments of anxiety. Preventing these small moments of joy can create stress and anxiety within you. It's also a double whammy, you didn't do the thing you craved for yourself so you feel frustrated at missing out, you also missed out on the relaxation that treat would have brought to you, so now you feel the double whammy effect on missing out. The flip side also applies, doing all those small treats and rewards can add up throughout the day. Instead of finishing the day feeling flat, stressed and deprived, you can finish the day feeling content and relaxed. You treated yourself to something and you gave yourself some time and care. Stress whether large or small can create anxiety, you can feel down, frustrated, upset and no matter how large or small the experience is, it can have an effect on your mind. Don't always assume that stress is a big event or incident. The big stressor moments are easy to spot, avoid or reflect upon. It's the small stressors in your life that can really build up and have an impact upon your day and mindset. They sneak up and build up without you ever noticing.

Stress within the mind can consume you, distract you and not allow you to function at the appropriate level. I cover this later in the book in more detail but the stress within your mind can then affect your body. Those aches, pains and sores can be related to stress within the body which has a source of stress within the mind. It's easy to dismiss stress as part of everyday life, and to some degree it is. Many years ago the stress response was to keep us safe from wild animals or other tribes, and to be honest these principles can still apply today in the modern world. Just replace a tribe from many many years ago with the workplace today where people will compete for job promotions to gain success and recognition. Whilst stress can keep us safe and help us perform better, for example the adrenaline rush that heightens our senses and allows us to perform at a higher level, but if this stress is too high, at an inappropriate time or we are in a constant state of stress then this will adversely affect us. Stress left unmanaged will build and build. It will affect your mind, mood and body. It will start to affect your performance at work, it will start to affect your judgement, it will start to affect your relationships.

Recognise the big moments or big events in your life that have or will create stress within you. Recognise these events. Give yourself time to prepare for them, give yourself time to process them, give yourself time to recover from them. Don't be the hero by constantly marching on, you'll just feel the negative effects later. Recognise the small moments in your life and day that bring you stress, give them the focus that they need. Most likely you're not even aware of them.

Zenquest:

Make a list of the different things that are on your mind over the past week. Mark them as little or big things and see where your stressors lie. Don't overthink it. Like all the tasks within this book, go with your intuition and right things down as they come to mind.

Let it flow out of you.

Zenbite:

Stress can come in all shapes and sizes, not just the obvious 'big' moments. Those little 'stressors' can build and build. Recognise them all and give yourself time to prepare, process and recover.

Chapter 2: Breathe

Many years I made a comment to my wife and brother, whilst walking around Washington DC very hungover, that was something like "how good is breathing." As I'm sure you can imagine there was a humorous response to my ridicule about such a strange and 'stupid' statement. I was in fact referring to the fact that I was extremely hungover and deep breathing in the cold winter air was transformative to the way I felt. Many years later I stand by this statement, maybe in very different circumstances and contexts but the theory still stands. Breathing is amazing. It's a part of life, without it we die. Simple as. There is no way around it that we have to breathe, it's a necessity to life. Breathing though, beyond just the usual every few seconds breath, in different situations can be amazing. My naive statement many years ago had referred to the cold air coming into my lungs, refreshing my body and also my mind, providing a sudden cold air feeling that awakened my dull and foggy mind from the alcohol my body had consumed the night before. This is pretty much the baseline for breathwork exercises that exist today.

Disclaimer: I'm not claiming I invented breathwork. Using your breath to help you in everyday situations, whether they are big or small, can be transformational to your mood and mindset. Take stress, when in a stressful situation simply taking a few deep breaths can clear your mind, reset your compass and remove a layer of anxiety from the situation. There will be countless studies that will prove scientifically why and how this works, but I'm not relying on that within this book. It simply works. Taking a deep breath when preparing, in the middle of or recovering from a stressful event is transformational. It provides your mind with a pause, it provides your body with an injection of life and it provides a level of relaxation to both your body and mind. It's a great technique throughout the day, in fact I can't really think of a situation where it's not useful. Unless maybe you're competing with your child in a 'hold your breath' competition. First thing in the morning, a 10-20 minute breathwork routine or just a few simple deep breaths can get you set for the day before you get out of bed. When you're getting ready in the morning, the rush is on to get where and when you need to be, taking a few deep breaths will calm the situation, even if you do it just as you leave through the door. Arguing with your (insert age) child to get ready for (insert destination), just pausing and taking a few deep breaths will calm you down and therefore them down. Stuck in traffic, take those deep breaths to reset the situation and reassess that things probably aren't that bad. Walking into an important meeting at work, meeting a new person for coffee, take a few deep breaths to calm and reset yourself. Before you go to sleep at night, a relaxing breathwork routine or again a few simple deep breaths will make the drift off to sleep that much easier. In fact I often use the technique with my 9 year old daughter who has an active mind, especially as it hits in the magic time for sleep. A few deep breaths with her, clears her mind, resets her body and allows her mind and body to relax, providing a platform to sleep.

Combining your breath with grounding can take your calmness to the next level. Whilst taking deep breaths simply imagine yourself anchoring to the ground. Choose whatever method feels comfortable. It could be energy running down your legs or spine in the form of a waterfall or a cord. Your feet feeling the ground or surface beneath you. Just make it a feeling of connecting to the ground or surface beneath you. A connection to something below and going down into the earth. This can sound a bit weird to begin with, don't worry I've been there. "Cord running to the centre of the earth, what?" Trust me once you wrap your head around it, grounding yourself along with your some deep breaths can really transform a situation. If you're preparing for an event or situation, say an important presentation at work or job interview, taking a few deep breaths and grounding your energy and body will bring a level of calmness into the situation. If you're knee deep in situation and the sh*t is hitting the fan and nothing is going to plan. Same thing, take a few deep breaths, ground yourself and continue. Once you've come out of a stressful or tiring event take the time to ground your energy, run that cord down, imagine your feet connecting to the floor, imagine a waterfall of energy running to the core of the earth, whatever works for you grounding yourself can bring you back into connection with your body and mind. Combining it with the magic breath techniques and stressful situations can be transformed. Give it a try, even now, just stop reading this book, take a few big deep breaths. In through the nose and out through the mouth, do a few…in…out….

I'll wait……

Feels good doesn't it.

Taking it to the next level with a specific breathwork course, that goes much deeper, can really explore parts of your mind that you never knew were there. Breathwork, which is a much deeper technique to inhale and exhale for a certain count and holding your breath goes much deeper in exploring the power of the breath. This is a much bigger topic that is covered by many experts and can provide a great relief for stress and exploring anxiety or stress within your life. I recommend everyone to investigate this further. In everyday life though a few simple deep breaths can really change your days.

Zenquest:
When you're in a stressful event or any event that creates a level of anxiety within you simply pause and take a few deep breaths. Extend this to add in grounding your energy and body to really bring a calmness to your mind.

Take this to the next level, find a breathwork course in your area or a video on YouTube to get into this practice.

Zenbite:

Your breath is one of the most powerful tools you possess.

Chapter 3: Balance

Balance is a word that can have different meanings to different people and in different contexts. There is physical balance, mental balance, work / life balance and more. All of these contexts are the balance of two opposing forces that are working 'against' each other. The yin and the yang. The masculine and the feminine. The rich and the poor. The dark and the light. The list goes on. In each of these instances, balance represents a harmonious coexistence of these opposing forces, creating a delicate equilibrium.

So why is balance important? Balance brings about the harmonisation of your mind and body. How many times have you not felt in tune with yourself, something is off, something's not quite right. You can get irritable, tired and grumpy and take it out on yourself and others. You are out of balance with yourself and the physical world around you. Balance is the outcome that enables us to find harmony across our lives. Without balance we can become stressed, anxious, ill and more. Feeling out of balance can create these moments of stress which on the surface seem harmless but can run deep into your mind, soul and body. Therefore having an impact on you and those around you. Some examples I often think include; health, it's great to eat a healthy diet but if that diet consists just of celery and you are depriving your body of the nourishment and nutrients that it needs then that is not good for your health, it will create stress on your body. On the other hand if you just eat everything in sight and anything you want then that is not healthy either, you will become overweight and stress will be created on your body. A balanced diet will create a healthy body and a healthy mind, eat the treats you like in moderation but don't overdo it. Another example is money. Saving all of your money is great as long as it doesn't stop you from doing the things you like to do. If all you do is save, save, save and you have a healthy bank balance, whilst this can ease your mind as your basic safety needs are being met, just think of all the things in life you are missing out on. You are missing out on experiences, adventures, time with others, possessions that you would like to purchase. This starts to build and creates anxiety within yourself as you are missing out on the joys of life and not getting the reward for all your efforts. On the other hand, spending all the money you have without any consideration of the consequences will create a life in which you have lots of things or have had lots of experiences but you have no safety net to fall back on. If hard times hit then you may suffer and feel the consequences of not saving any money. It can also work away in the back of your mind, your mind knows that you don't have the safety net in place and whilst you're enjoying all of these amazing things there is a safety that is missing. This creates a level of anxiety within you that you may not even know is there. Therefore, spending in moderation to enjoy life whilst also saving is a way to have balance within your finances.

Once you find the balance your mind will feel relaxed and therefore your body will feel relaxed. It's about finding the balance for yourself. Everyone is different and it's not about getting everything 50/50, that's just not the way life works, it's about finding the balance that works for you and what feels right for you. It's not an exact science, but once you find that balance you will feel it. That's the important part. It will bring you contentment and calm. Your world feels in harmony, things just work, things just happen, things feel good. You have brought balance to your life. I'm not going to cover every single area of your life in which you can get out of balance, but look for areas of your life that aren't quite flowing, they feel off, and not right, that is your inner compass telling you that something you are experiencing isn't right. Listen to it, it's your inner intuition trying to guide you. Finding balance can be simple and sometimes it can be tricky as it may require some changes and adjustments to your life that may require some big changes. You know your current relationship or job isn't for you, breaking away can be simple and easy but other times it can be more complex and feel hard as there are lots of factors involved. The key is to start taking the first steps, make some simple changes, and start to work towards the changes that you need in your life. Sometimes though a big shift will be required to change your patterns and routines to bring your life back into balance. Once you do though you will feel it. It will feel right and your life will start to feel easier as everything feels in the right place at the right time.

Zenquest:
Think of the areas within your life, from money, health, relationships, work, family and growth. Rate each area to see how balanced you feel. Go with your intuition, don't overthink it, just put down a number between 1-10. This will start to give you some insight into where you are feeling good and areas where you don't quite feel right.

Zenbite:

Balance is important to create harmony across your life and allow it to flow

Chapter 4: Flow

Ah being in flow, sounds good doesn't it, but what does that actually mean? Being in flow is having the ability to go with the flow of life, not to think too hard, trust your intuition and see where it will take you. First you need to clear your mind from all the noise, keep it simple and go with your heart with what feels right. Most of the time the first thing that pops into your head is the right decision, it's only when we over analyse that we start to 'mess with the flow'. We procrastinate, we doubt ourselves, we just simply think too much. We start to make decisions that aren't based on our intuition, instead they are based upon a bunch of other things that enter our minds, what will this person think, what will happen if I do that, it's too hard, I'm not good enough. Going with the flow is seeing where life takes you. Whether you believe in some divine power or simply trust that YOU know what is best for YOU. Why should someone else know what is better for you? Sure get inputs from your surroundings and those around you but it should be you who makes the decision. You are the one who has to deal with the consequences of your life. Going with the flow makes life feel fun and probably a little scary. Scary can be good sometimes, though it means you are pushing your boundaries and going out of your comfort zone. If your body is screaming nooooooo! Like a clear big resounding NO, then it's probably not the right thing to do, however if it feels like the right decision but is a little scary, and maybe the no is a quiet no, then it's probably the right thing to do, you're just pushing your boundaries and your mind isn't too sure about things as it's going out of it's comfort zone. This is a good thing. It may feel like you're relinquishing control but in fact it's the opposite you're actually going with your intuition, you are in control not an overactive mind that has been overly influenced by others or your surroundings. When you get into the flow and trust your intuition it can be a great feeling, things just, well flow, they feel right, things happen that make sense. You may feel lighter and stronger all at the same time. You may even feel like someone is on your side helping you out. Again, you may believe that there is a greater power at work and you are following your pre-destined path, I personally don't hold this belief but I don't judge others that do. Others will feel like it's just life flowing their way, there doesn't have to be a greater power at work. Being connected to your thoughts and feelings, whether they are internally generated or from a greater source, either way you are following what is true to you and going with the flow. Deep down you know what is best for you and if you let it follow your intuition, it can take you to great places. Just remember part of being in the flow is not overthinking things, it's going with that gut feeling.

This can take some trust. Not all of us have the ability to trust, whether it be in our nature or from past experiences. The person you are trusting however is yourself. This can sound hard depending upon your circumstances. If you've never trusted yourself before or you have trusted what you thought was right only for it to backfire in your face, "I thought I was doing the right thing!" Everything you do may have felt like it turned into a nightmare, but everything is not a nightmare. Sitting in traffic is not a nightmare, spilling your coffee on your new jeans is not a nightmare. Being lost in a forest at night with no phone, torch or anything and the dark has closed in fast and you are wandering aimlessly to god knows where and you are truly lost - that's kind of a nightmare. But back to reality, being in flow is about trusting yourself deep down, really clearing your mind and removing all the noise that is around you. Once you get deep down you will feel what is right to do. Make the decision and see how your mind and body feel. Trust your body as it's a big barometer for the mind and soul. If your body doesn't feel right then something is off. Maybe the decision you made isn't the right one. Try again and see how it feels. Turn off your mind a little and see where your intuition takes you. Check in with yourself to see how you feel, feel weird. Stop. Feel right, carry on. Go with the flow.

One aspect that can improve your 'going with the flow' is being grounded.If you're grounded and feeling strong then your mind will feel safe too and be more comfortable relinquishing control. It's about connecting to the earth, you may believe you are connecting to an underlying network or power. You may believe that you are channeling the energy of the earth. You may not believe any of that. You know what, it doesn't matter. If it works, why question it. Ground yourself by imagining energy flowing down your body, feet and arms into the earth. Take your shoes off for an added bonus. Feel the energy flow down, take some deep breaths, pause and just listen to the world around you, especially if you're in nature, if not try and listen out for the birds, insects and wildlife that are always around us. Pause, breath and let the energy flow into the ground.

Like I say, you may believe there is a greater power at work or you may not. It doesn't matter, the act of grounding yourself, taking a minute, breathing and feeling into your body will make you feel calm and connected. Being grounded will enhance your intuition and flow even more, it will bring a calm to your mind and body, it will make you feel connected to yourself and your surroundings bringing a level of trust and safety.

Zenquest:

Think of a time when you didn't go with the flow, you over thought and analysed things. How did it go? Did it feel right? Did the experience flow?

When a decision comes up next, try grounding yourself and then make the decision and see how it feels.

Zenbite:

Go with the flow of life and see where the magic takes you.

Chapter 5: Intuition

Throughout this book intuition will come up a lot, it has already. Intuition is the source of your greatest guidance. You can listen to others, read books and seek help from others but ultimately when the decision has to be made the best guide is yourself. What is intuition? It's the inner being within you that knows how you truly feel. It's your soul, it's your spirit. At the end of the day it's you who knows what is best for you. Don't get me wrong, you can certainly learn from others in terms of their experiences and wisdom. People have great things to share, some of them will be relevant and some may not, but listen to others and take on board what they have to say. The same can be said for gathering information about a decision, reading books, listening to podcasts, searching the internet and using this information to broaden your scope of information on a topic. There are great sources out there to expand your knowledge in an area and allow you to make a more informed decision. But after all, and any sources, have been reviewed, the important part is to do what you believe in, don't do what others believe in or what others think you should do, this isn't true to yourself. This is the important part of intuition. Your mind has gathered information from a wide variety of sources with information coming into your senses consciously and unconsciously all the time. Many things that shape your views you're probably not even aware of but they are shaping how you see and perceive the world. You are the most important person in your life, the airplane videos are true, you need to help yourself before you can help others. Listen to what is true to you through your intuition and follow your heart and soul. For example when you order a meal at a restaurant and deep down you know it's going to suck, but you ordered it anyway hoping it would be good but it's not. You don't know why you thought that, but you did and you were right, you should have trusted your intuition. This is just a small impact with little or no impact but your intuition or ignoring your intuition can have greater consequences when the stakes are higher. Say you are offered a promotion at work, you know your heart isn't in it, you have found a much more rewarding but lower paid role that makes you feel good about yourself. Your intuition is screaming take the sh*t paid job, take it, take it, your current job is just more of the same but with more money but surrounded by idiots. You ignore your intuition and take the promotion. Six months later you are in what can only be described as a meeting from hell, your life is oozing away in front of your very eyes. "Why am I sitting here with these people?" You then flash back to that decision and look at your fancy new laptop and iPhone, was it really worth it? You should have trusted your intuition.

It can sound hard to put yourself first, I can't just do what I want, I have responsibilities. The most important thing you can do in your life is to be true to yourself and follow your intuition. Your intuition is the gut feeling, the burning desire, the feeling when something feels right or doesn't feel right. That is your soul saying whether you are on the right or wrong path. It can be hard to hear it sometimes as the world is a noisy place. Lots of stimulation and lots of information is being sent out into the world all of the time and it can be hard to get those quiet moments. I often find that in meditation, in whatever form that may take for you, is when your intuition can shine. Meditation is a term I use loosely, to me meditation is that act of clearing your mind and being present. That could be sitting still, on a walk through nature, painting, doing the dishes, going on a run, practising yoga. It's the time when your mind is clear and focused away from the noise of the world and others. It's the time when you feel calm. It's important to allow these experiences within your life as that's when the noise of the world is less and your intuition can shine through. You are in your own bubble, a good bubble, where your thoughts can be expressed freely. Sometimes your intuition won't sound right, I can't do that there will be impacts on other people. But it's that burning feeling that you know something is true. If everything else was removed what would you do in a situation, remove all the barriers and what does your soul want to do. Not following your intuition can make you feel off balance, something doesn't feel right because your soul is screaming at you that this is not the path for you. Learning from others and gathering information is a key part to life but listening to yourself is the most important aspect to living a life that you are true to yourself.

Balance, flow and intuition are all intertwined. They are connected and rely on each other. Trust your intuition and you will find balance, once you find balance things in your life will flow.

Zenquest:
Think of a time when you didn't listen to your intuition, what was the outcome? Think of a time when you did,

how did it differ?

Zenbite:

Follow your intuition it knows what is best for you

Chapter 6: Symbiotic

The mind is a powerful thing, it controls our emotions, moves our body, controls our thoughts, allows us to process information and emotions, it pretty much controls everything within our body. This is the important part - it has control over everything within our body. Therefore the state of our mind controls the state of our body and vice versa. If we feel stressed, in our minds, this will manifest throughout our body. The classic examples being heart attacks, strokes, panic attacks due to long term stress. Our mind wields its power over our body. If our mind is stressed the body thinks hey what's going on something bad may be about to happen so goes into survival mode and puts our body into a state of stress, ready to react. Likely originating from thousands of years ago when we were hunter gatherers, if a tiger was approaching, our mind saw the danger and put our body into a state of stress so we could respond i.e. Run away as fast we can into the hills screaming. In today's world, in most cases, we don't have this danger but it's been replaced by perceived danger. It's important to note, perceived danger not actual danger. Our minds stress about a whole range of things, work, relationships, kids, traffic, money, the list goes on. Our mind is therefore in a constant state of stress and in reaction to this puts our body to work to react accordingly. Why is it that a long day at work leaves your body feeling exhausted? You didn't move all day, but you're physically exhausted. Your mind has been working all day so your body feels tired to be in tandem with your mind. It's common knowledge that stress can impact your body, examples of some physical ailments of stress are acne, a sore back, headaches are just a few. Therefore by simple logic by reducing our mental stress we can also reduce the stress on our bodies. We can create mechanisms to remove or cope with the mental stress, that in turn alleviates the stress put onto our bodies. The two are very much interlinked.

On the flip side, a body in poor condition will also affect the mind. An unhealthy body will create an unhealthy mind. A tired body can create a tired mind. Things feel physically hard, this translates into things feeling mentally hard. "I'm tired I can't be bothered" how many times have you said this or heard someone else say it. The stress on our body creates stress on our mind. We want to achieve a physical goal, say go on a 5km run through the park, but our body is not fit enough, we can't make it and give up. It impacts upon our mind, we failed, our body failed, our mind now thinks we've failed. If there was a lion running through the park we would be mincemeat by now. The two are closely linked. If we eat too much junk food our bodies feel heavy, we feel sluggish, everything feels physically hard. That starts to translate into other areas, your body is being stressed by all the junk food it's consuming. It feels tired, it's working hard to process the junk, you're carrying too much weight. Now your mind joins in, "hey I'm tired too body. Maybe let's just do nothing." You end up in a downward spiral of getting more and more unhealthy physically and now more and more unhealthy mentally.

However, as the mind has control over the body we can utilise this to our advantage. When our body gets injured, our mind mans the troops and sends the relevant defence forces to repair the body. After a few days that cut you had on your leg is healed due to your body healing itself, which is controlled and triggered by the mind. Our body tells the mind we are injured, "hey mind I fell over and banged my leg, looks like we'll need some work done here". The mind in turn reacts "don't worry about it, I'll send some troops down to get things sorted. You might be out of action for a few days so just give it time". The body sends down the appropriate cells to repair the body - they are in a symbiotic relationship. All this time you consciously did nothing to activate or be part of this process. Your mind and body working together "don't worry we've got this". They go to work and repair your body with no conscious thought required from you. It's all down subconsciously and automatically. You were just along for the ride.

Therefore if the body can automatically heal itself, why can't we take this concept of unconscious healing to create conscious healing? Why can't we instruct the mind to heal our body? We have a sore back, we do need to get to the underlying cause of the sore back. It could have been a physical injury but it also could be stress building up in our mind and that's where our body has decided to deposit the stress. There is a theory that the placement of this physical pain is specific to each part of the body, for example a sore hand will indicate a specific emotion that you're experiencing or not experiencing and that's where the body will store the stress. So we do need to get to the underlying cause of the stress to resolve it, otherwise it will just return and more likely even more painful. However, we can also instruct our minds to send the appropriate cells to help heal our body to speed up our recovery. We can heal the mind first, remove any blocks, stress and issues that we have created. Doing so we can remove the initial cause of the stress and we can also instruct our bodies to go and heal that part of our body and to focus on that part of the body to heal it. Fix the mind, fix the body. Use your mind to help speed up the recovery process. We may also have a physical injury that our body is already taking care of, let's help it out by telling our mind to focus on this area of the body to send extra help. This concept can apply to heal physical ailments caused by stress, injuries or long term trauma. Again we need to clear and heal the mind and then tell our bodies to go to work to heal itself and focus on a specific area. As we go through life it's important to recognise this relationship between your mind and body and how they interact and relate to each other. Appreciating the impact they have on each other can help us understand more about our lifestyle and state of mind to lead a more relaxed and fulfilled life.

Zenquest:
Think of a time you were stressed, mentally stressed, how did your body feel? Did it feel good or did it feel

tired and sore? Next time you feel stress, notice the impact upon your body.

Think of a physical ailment you would like to heal. Start to think positive thoughts on that part of your body to start healing. See what happens over the next few weeks.

Zenbite:

The mind and body have a symbiotic relationship.

REFLECT

Chapter 7: Appreciate

Looking at what you have in your life is important to recognise what you have achieved, where you are at, your accomplishments and not taking what you have for granted. If you don't recognise what you have and appreciate it then you will never be happy. This doesn't mean you can't dream or set high goals, it means to recognise what you have and the achievements that you have made. It may not be perfect, hey nothing is perfect and that's totally fine. Life's variety lies within the imperfections. If everything or everybody was perfect life would be boring. Set those goals, manifestations and milestones but be grateful for what you have achieved and how far you have come. Otherwise you will never appreciate what you have now and what your new goal will provide you in the future. You will simply achieve your new goal but then be looking at what's next. Enjoy the journey and absorb what is around you. I don't think it's a coincidence that some of the happiest people on earth are often those from what are seen as 'poorer' countries, they appreciate the simplest of life and their connection to others and nature. Appreciating these connections around you provides contentment within your life. You have achieved great things. Many of us don't believe this to be true, but having a job, a family, helping a friend, raising a child are all great achievements. We aren't trained to see these things as achievements but they are. Some of the hardest things in life are not recognised as achievements as they may occur to everyone. Holding down a job is an achievement, teaching a child to read is an achievement, finishing school is an achievement, providing support to a friend who is in need is an achievement, raising a family is an achievement. We often sweep these achievements under the carpet, it's just part of life, everyone does it. That may be true but it's still an achievement, you have shown up in life to be there for yourself or another person. You didn't have to. Doing so is an achievement in itself. Appreciate the things and people in your life. Appreciate the situation you are in, what can you learn, what have you learned through the process. Look back and see what you have achieved, in the good and bad we can find inspiration. This is often forgotten.

Look around you now or later today and really soak up what is good in your life. The birds singing in the trees, your family's health, the joy on your children's faces from a simple activity together, the green leaves, the blue in the sky, the sun on your face. Many of us will have adversities in our lives; health, family, wealth the list goes on. However, appreciating what you do have will help you set your goals in life. It will help you reduce stress, it will help you find some balance. Things may not seem great but looking for the positive in things and what is around you will bring some sense of happiness and appreciation that will bring balance to you and those around you. Passing on this appreciation to others is important, setting the example for your children to appreciate things in life will set them up for a more fulfilling life. Seeing the cup as half full not half empty will inspire you to go further to fill the rest of that cup. Be grateful for those who are around you and any time that they spend with you. Connection is important and shows your appreciation to others. Everyone is just a human being stepping their way through life and trying to do their best.

Appreciating what you have will allow you to move forward with purpose and strength. It will provide a feeling of stability. I have a great life, I can make it even better but I have a great life now. Again, that doesn't mean don't set your goals, but appreciate what you have achieved and what you are going to achieve otherwise you will never find happiness, you will always be looking for something more or looking back thinking things weren't good enough. Appreciate the large and small things in life. That simple cup of tea in the morning, the sunset, the fresh crunchy apple. It's often the small things that matter the most and will fill your day with joy. A day filled with joy, will spread to a week of joy, to a month of joy, to a full year of joy that you can reflect on and appreciate the experiences you have had. How you view what you have in your life can affect your mindset, let's say you invest $1000 in the stock market. After 6 months the value of the stocks has risen to $2000, you've doubled your money and have a $1000 return on the investment. Now, say you leave the investment and after 12 months it's now worth $1500. There are two ways to view this; you have gained $500 on the $1000 invested, or you lost $500 as it was worth $2000 6 months earlier. See the gain, not the loss. Sure it was worth $2000 but now it's worth $1500 and you started with $1000, take the win and see what you gained. If you focus on the perceived loss then you will see the investment as a negative, not as the positive return that you have made. This applies to areas of your life, appreciate what you have, appreciate what you have gained in life. Acknowledge the losses and how you have learned from them, but see the gains you have made from the experience or interaction.

Enjoy the journey. Look around, breathe in your surroundings, look at the colours around you, the people around. Look at what you have achieved, look at what you are achieving every day. Even in the most simple ways you are achieving great things. This can vary per person, for someone landing a big deal at work is a great achievement, for someone else it can simply be getting out of bed that day. Achievements are relative to the person, don't constantly compare yourself, sure look to your heroes or role models for inspiration, but judge your achievements on yourself not what others have achieved. Often if someone else excels in an area that you're not good at, you will excel in other areas. It's all relative to you. Enjoy the journey, the experiences you have, the people you meet, the food you eat, and simply the air your breath. In every experience there is something to learn, something that can be viewed as negative is actually an opportunity to learn.

If you are constantly looking at the end goal, once you achieve that goal, what next? Another goal? The next big thing. That doesn't mean not to have goals but enjoy the journey towards those goals. If you are enjoying the journey then life is one big adventure with learning and achievements along the way. Celebrate the achievements, you worked hard, you dedicated time, energy and effort but enjoy the journey more. Don't pin all your hopes on a specific outcome, things can change, life does change. Change is great, change creates variety in life. If you strive towards a fixed highly defined goal, when that goal changes, then what? Have a goal in mind but be open to how you achieve it. Don't focus on the how, that will come through balance and intuition and the synchronisation of life. Let go and go with the flow, combine this with balance and intuition to enjoy the journey. Take time to look around you and take it all in, it's a classic statement, but I believe those classic statements are generally true for a reason, because well they are true. Take deep breaths, slow down to appreciate things as they fly by. Allow yourself to appreciate what you have and be grateful for what you have and are achieving.

Zenquest:
Make a list of all the great things you have achieved in your life and the great things in your life today.

Zenbite:
Look around you, breathe in and take in what you have in your life. This is the path to true happiness and

growth.

Chapter 8: Treat others well

This may sound like a strange one, but treat others like it's the last time you may see them. That doesn't mean to give them a huge tearful hug and let them know your dying wishes every time you say goodbye, it's about how you would feel if that was the last time you saw a person when you said goodbye. Did you part on good terms or were there harsh words? Did you scream at them as they left the house for the day or did you give them a loving hug? Did you say something that later you regretted when the heat of the moment had passed or did you leave them with kind words?

The principle of this concept is imagine something happened to those who are close to you and also those that aren't close to you. It sounds a little dramatic but what if your husband was in a severe car crash on the way to work, your teenager child got hit by a bus on the way to school. The pain of loss is already unimaginable when something happens to someone you love. Take that pain and multiply it if the last experience you had with them was negative. The slam of the door as you left the house, the harsh words as you hung up the phone. Those final moments will extend the pain of losing a loved one knowing that your final words were ones of hurt. This is the basis of this principle, treat others as if it was the last time you would see them. See them with love and forgive their actions. Are those harsh and critical words really how you feel about that person? Look at those moments of goodbye as moments to cherish, what if it was the last time you saw this person in your life. This extends to those who you may not be close to, colleagues at work, the guy in the coffee shop, the annoying woman from accounts who's always on your back and you don't have any kind words to say about. How would you feel if your last encounter with them was one of negativity and harsh words, then something happened to them and they were never to return. Even though it may not be a close relationship, would you be happy with how you treated them, were those harsh words worth it? Were those harsh thoughts worth it?

It's similar to 'treat others as how you would like to be treated yourself', but extending this to really comprehend what if it was the last time you saw this person, would you be comfortable and content with your last experiences. Everyone, at the end of the day, is a person trying to make their way in the world. It could be said that this principle is to make yourself feel better, and to be honest it is, but the actions that follow this way of thinking are those of kindness and compassion that extends to others, not just yourself. Allowing you to treat those around you with respect and compassion. See the situation and person as a whole, not just in isolation. Yes they may have wronged you but you can forgive them or see the situation from their perspective. Most people aren't vindictive or harsh, they are going through the day doing the best that they can in their own way. Sure they might have not been kind but it's based upon what they have learnt, their previous experiences and what they are currently experiencing. Maybe that person who just cut you up in traffic is trying to get home to see their sick child, the checkout worker is so slow because they haven't eaten all day as they couldn't afford any lunch. See others for who they are and the situation they are in, show them compassion. It could be the last time and only time you see this person, how would you feel about your interaction with them. This doesn't mean to cave in to their every need or not stand your ground, if there is a negative experience with someone hold yourself with honour and compassion. Show kindness and forgiveness when others can't. If you act in this way towards others, then they will start to learn the same behaviour whether it's consciously or unconsciously. Maybe your small act of kindness will pass onto them, the consideration you give them will enhance their day and they will pass it onto others.

This way of approaching others and your interaction with them creates a chain reaction, when you spend time with them and say your goodbyes. Do it with compassion and love, it will enrich their experience with you and therefore enrich their day. They will move into the world with a sense of contentment and compassion which they will hopefully pass onto others. Imagine the opposite, when you leave someone with harsh words, you feel bad, they feel bad and you both go into the world feeling bad and likely pass this onto those around you. Say you're on the bus on the way to work in an angry mood, someone else may consciously or subconsciously feel the rage coming from you. It could be the receptionist at your office who feels the cold shoulder as you enter the building. This negative energy from your parting experience is taken out of that experience and into the world and passes to others who are totally unaware of the situation. Some people are very sensitive to others feelings, even if they aren't the recipient of those words, they can feel them from a distance, they can pick up on the bad vibes and this indirectly affects their day. So as you leave a situation, do us all a favour and leave it in a positive light and frame of mind. Instead of creating negativity for you, the recipient and those who come into contact with you, create an environment of positivity that will leave you, others and the recipient in a clear and positive state of mind. If something happened to that person who you just interacted with, you can go with some peace in that your interaction with them was one of positivity not negativity. Again, it's a little strange way of looking at things but it's about treating others with respect and compassion and allowing that to pass on into the world.

Zenquest:

Think of a time when you've left a situation with someone and you've been really mad at them. How would you feel if that was the last time you saw them? Would it change the way you engaged with them when you left?

Zenbite:

Life throws us curve balls, treat others with love and respect.

Chapter 9: Little things

The little things matter in life, initially it might not seem that way but all those small things that you think don't really matter really do add up. Take a new top of the range phone, say an iPhone, sure there are other phones that are cheaper and better value for money but with an iPhone it's all the little things that add up. It all just works, the animations that give it a polished feel, the fact that you're looking for a setting and it's naturally in the place you expect, the feel of the case. All of these small design decisions add up to an overall great product. This can be applied to your life, all the little things that you do and experience are important. The little things do really matter in life. These can come in the form of helping someone, putting in that little bit of extra effort to your work, being early for an appointment, not rushing something and taking just that little bit longer to make sure it's done right, all these things often add up to big things.

Take IKEA furniture, I can honestly say every time I put together a piece of IKEA furniture it's a chore. What seems like a small task, invariably ends up taking

5 times longer. It's not that the instructions are poor, or the quality of the product is poor. You just take a look at the table in the store, or on the site and think I'll have that done in 30 minutes, 3 hours later you finally complete the task. I'm not sure why it is, but the universe says IKEA furniture (and any similar self-built furniture brand) should take at least 5 times longer than you think. There is an equation in the universe and fabric of time which only allows this. Never is a piece of IKEA furniture assembled in less time than you plan. Whilst assembling the furniture you start off slow, reading all the instructions, but after sometime you start to speed up, yes I know what I'm doing, I've done this 8 times already, as I'm on the 8th leg of a 10 leg table. You reach near the end, you've done it, you've survived, wait why won't this attach, why is that not aligned? You go back 35 pages of the 56 page manual to discover in a moment of early confidence you attached a piece incorrectly. At the time, and the subsequent next 21 pages all seemed fine. But no, alas that small incorrect mistake has now changed the course of the whole furniture and you have to face the inevitable that you will need to dismantle the whole thing to rectify your mistake. Take this analogy into your life, a small insignificant act can change the course of your life, that

little thing that you did or didn't do has an effect. You buy your partner a small gift, say a box of their favourite chocolates, they were having a bad day, they thought no one cared, but this little seemingly small gesture changes their day, it brightens it up and allows them to see you and their day in a different light. They notice other small tasks you do for them, before you know it they are appreciating the things that you did and see you in a better light. Obviously, this can work the other way around. You don't do the small gesture, in fact you do the opposite and expect them to do something for you, you're being lazy, this festers within them and grows, they start to notice the other annoying habits and it grows and grows. That little gesture you didn't do grows into a level of resentment which is much larger. The little things when combined together or on top of each other can have a great effect. Take the trajectory of a rocket ship, if after takeoff the course of the rocket is very slightly affected by just a few degrees it's destination will greatly change, ending up kms away from its intended destination. The culmination of little decisions can have a huge impact on your life, the lives of others and the world as a whole.

A child who receives consistent little positive

reinforcement will learn that the behaviour is positive. Those little reinforcements can make a big change in their lives and shape their lives and how they interact with others, therefore changing the lives of others around them. The combination of all the little things in life shouldn't be underestimated. Little decisions can affect the trajectory of your life or someone else's, resulting in a large change in the world and other lives. That doesn't mean to overthink every single little decision and start to procrastinate, but don't dismiss the importance of little things in life. Appreciate their impact. So what does this mean, do you need to analyse every little thing you do? No, just be aware that the little things count and when combined can contribute to create something great or on the flip side something not so great. Not doing all those little things that either add a benefit to yourself or someone else can add up. Maybe you don't give yourself that extra 5 minutes to get ready, you end up rushing everyday, every single day you rush just to make the train to work. This creates stress and anxiety within you and puts you in rush mode all morning. Maybe just take time to get up 5 minutes earlier to remove that rush, it's a minor thing but could change your whole mood for the day. Going for a walk for 15-30 minutes a day at lunchtime, adds up to overall better health. The classic take the stairs instead of the elevator, it all adds up to have a greater impact upon your life than the single act itself. The little things really do matter and can really change your life, the actions you take can transform your day. It might feel hard to do that little task, but deep down you know it's the right thing to do, and when you do it you reap the rewards of feeling better from the direct outcome but you also get a sense of achievement, again that may be small but it all adds up.

Great things come from little things.

Zenquest:
Take something you like, a piece of clothing, a tech of technology, a person you know. List out all the little things about this object or person that you like. See all the little things that combine to make you like this person or product.

Zenbite:
Just because something seems little it doesn't mean it's impact can't be great.

Chapter 10: Cherish the moments

Moments in life can pass you by without you realising their importance, the small things or maybe even the big things that you don't truly soak in. It could be something big, like your wedding day. How many people say the day just passes without them pausing to appreciate the day. How many birthdays, days out, holidays just pass you by without you really, I mean really, soaking in the moment and really appreciating the moment that you are in. Taking a step back and enjoying what is in front of you. This is sometimes easier in those big obvious life changing moments as you can recognise them as major events in your life. Maybe someone did tell you to enjoy your wedding day so you took the time to stand still and observe. On a special birthday you surveyed the room and really took in those family and friends that had joined you to celebrate. Sometimes we are lucky to remember and be aware of the moment and take in what is happening around us. Seeing those around us, feeling their emotions, feeling our own emotions, taking in our surroundings and appreciating the moment. This doesn't just apply to big events in your life, they are often easier to take stock of because you register the importance of the day, you take that step back and observe. These are important moments to savour, they hold a special meaning to your life and those around you. They are likely life defining moments and you can recognise them if you give yourself a chance to stop and take it all in. Take in all the faces around you and the way you and those around you are feeling. More than likely it's a good day, one to remember. Just make sure you take the time to take it in.

Whilst the big moments are important, the little moments can be just as or even more important to the flow and fulfilment of your life. Watching the sunset, playing with the kids, taking the dog for a walk on a perfect autumn day when the temperature and light are just perfect, having a nice cup of tea in your favourite armchair. Taking in these seamless meaningless everyday things are just as important as the big events. Sure, those big events shape and change your life, they set you off on a new direction that will change the direction of your life. You can see the importance of the day so you take stock that this is a once in a lifetime event. You acknowledge that it's an event that will shape the direction of your life and those around you.

Cherish the moments

Those small events though, those every day, minor moments are the ones that can really shape your life without you ever knowing. The major moments can be in your conscious, the minor moments are working in your subconscious, they are evolving your thoughts and visions without you ever knowing. They are shifting and changing the person you are. Enjoy these moments. The sun sets every day, sometimes it's not great but other days it can be incredible. Stop, take in the moment. The kids playing in the garden, those moments won't last forever. Sitting on the sofa snuggled together watching a movie, take those moments in. They may happen all of the time, and sometimes you think it will happen tomorrow so I don't need to take the time to enjoy them, but then again they may not. You can make everyday amazing, you just need to take it in and cherish the moments. They shape your mood, they shape your energy, they shift your mind and body. If you appreciate those moments your stress can drop, you are being grateful for life and any worries can melt away even just for a split second. That split second can count, your brain registers it. It takes that event and stores it with the good memories. These small seemingly significant positive events happen everyday and before you know it you are storing these amazing everyday moments all the time and you begin to cherish life that little bit more. It gives you an appreciation for what is around you and the experiences you are having. As you do this everyday your appreciation grows for life, you appreciate and are grateful for those around you. You cherish life more and it starts to bring you everyday happiness. You just need to cherish those daily moments.

Everyday bliss is a great goal to have in life. To appreciate and cherish those moments, to be truly grateful for life, dismiss negative thoughts and focus on the positive experiences and people in your life. You will find yourself smiling everyday, and that can truly be one of life's great medicines. The negative times will come, they will allow us to grow and learn from them, but turn them into a positive and cherish the learnings that they give you. In this way you can begin to cherish the good and bad times in your life. The bad times will come, they may be really bad or just bad, but everyone will go through some level of tough time. It's just part of life and creates an opportunity to learn and grow, although it may not seem that way at the time. Shift your mindset to even cherish these moments, they may be negative on the surface but there's always something positive to take away. These moments allow you to grow as a person, you learn something new about yourself or others. Cherish these moments as ultimately positive and you can really appreciate all aspects of life and it's incredible journey.

Zenquest:

Think of 5 everyday positive moments that you have experienced today that you may have overlooked. Go back, how did they make you feel?

Zenbite:

Cherish the simple everyday moments in life.

Chapter 11: Forgiveness

To really live a life of peace, calm and kindness, forgiveness is a key part to allow you to really achieve this. Without it you will not be able to fully fulfil your potential, you will be clouded by thoughts and judgements that we cannot let go of. Forgiveness doesn't mean to forget, it doesn't mean it won't hurt anymore, these things will take time but it means you have forgiven someone and can begin to move on with your life. Holding onto something and not forgiving someone can take over your life. When you forgive someone the pain is still there but it no longer controls you, you will never forget it but you are able to move on with your life. Some things will be easy to forgive, the small annoyances in life like the rude cashier in the store or the person who cut you up in traffic. These are things that are easier to forgive and move on. Other things, as I'm sure you know, can be much harder to forgive. They are the deep seated experiences you've had, you have been wronged, betrayed or hurt. These experiences can take much longer to forgive as they run much deeper and have often been inflicted by those closest to us. However, if we are unable to forgive we will continue to harbour the hurt and negative feelings. Process the feelings, analyse the situation, but let them out or tell the person how you feel. No good can come from holding onto the negative feelings. Holding onto negative feelings just creates resentment, you can't move on, you're stuck in the past feelings and the past experience. The pain is still there, you feel it every day and it drags you down everyday. You think things over in your mind, over and over again. Why did they do that? Why did they say that? It hurt. Holding onto the experience just creates negative energy that courses through your body and begins to affect you in other ways. The negative energy creates stress and anxiety within you, this builds until your body can no longer tolerate it. Sometimes this can result in a minor physical ailment such as a sore back but other times the result could be something much larger such as panic attacks. To forgive doesn't mean to forget. If someone wrongs you, you can forgive them but you don't need to forget and allow them to do the same action again. Forgiveness allows you to process the experience, release any negative feelings and move on. You may start to see the person in a different light. The hurt may still be there but letting go will mean you don't have to experience and relive it every day.

Sometimes people struggle with forgiveness because they believe they have let the other person win. However, if you are still holding onto negative feelings it's you who is the one being punished. You are punishing yourself and the experience is continuing to punish you again and again. Process the experience, learn from it and express the feelings but let them go through forgiveness. There is no good that can come from holding onto those feelings and not forgiving someone. Often the person who caused you harm was and is hurting inside themselves, as they say 'hurt people hurt people'. Bullies are often hurting inside and have their own traumas they are dealing with. This can be something simple to something serious. Someone may have inflicted hurt on you because they feel hurt and want someone else to feel their own pain. These people are in pain, we should feel sorry for them and help them not hate them. Once you start on the path of forgiveness it doesn't automatically mean all the hurt will go away. You don't just forgive someone and hey presto all the anger and hurt is gone. It's a process, it's a journey. The hurt will linger, it will persist, there will be good and bad days. The first step to removing the hurt is forgiveness. By forgiving you start the process of healing. Without forgiveness the hurt will just persist and even grow stronger. You can start the healing journey. It may take some time and there may be tough days but taking that first step to forgiveness is clear. It will release the weight of the experience and negative feelings. Once you forgive you can begin to move on and release the hold that the experience or person has on you. It will make your mind and therefore your body feel lighter. Your mind will feel free. You will feel free.

Forgiveness also applies to yourself. We've all done things that we regret. Said something to a friend out of spite, shouted at our child or lashed out when we are feeling tired. These feelings can be just as bad, if not even worse, than negative feelings inflicted onto us by others. When you hurt someone, you were the one in control, you feel guilty, you didn't mean it and now you feel remorse and you punish yourself. The first step to resolve the guilt you have inflicted on yourself or onto others is to forgive yourself. Only then can you really be empathic. We are all human and making mistakes is part of life. Give yourself a break. Understand why you made the decision or action, forgive yourself and then speak to the other person. Sometimes we can be harsh on ourselves without anyone else being involved, we made a mistake, that inner critic, why did I do that?

Why did I say that? We all make mistakes, it's how you react and move on from the mistake.

Forgiveness is the first step, if you hold onto a grudge with a person or are carrying around anger towards someone or yourself it will consume your mind and it will also start to take over your body. The pain and anger will be collected by your body and it will create stress. This could be localised to somewhere, like a bad back or sore neck or it could work away at your immune system. You don't sleep enough as things run through your mind, you get run down and then start to get sick. The key to relieving this stress on yourself is clearing any anger and forgiving the person or yourself. It will seem hard but it is the first step to moving forward with your life and not lingering in the past.

Zenquest:
Think of someone who has wrong or upset you. Have you forgiven them? If not, what are you gaining by not forgiving the person? Would things be better for you (and them) if you forgave them?

Zenbite:
Forgiveness starts a path to healing. Without forgiveness there is just ongoing pain that can get

worse. Forgive yourself and forgive others, we are all human and make mistakes.

Chapter 12: Nothing is perfect

P erfection means different things to different people but the principle is the same. Whether it be work, relationships, hobbies, the need to perfect things, to get things right and to tick all the boxes. Striving for perfection is not a bad thing, it drives us forward, it motivates us to carry on when things aren't going to plan or not complete. It pushes us forward and keeps up our momentum. We look to improve things and take them to the next level, to find the perfect person, the perfect fit, the perfect job. Striving for perfection can be seen within sport, the minor changes can combine to make a big difference, the team works together to perfect the race car or a sportsman perfecting and practising their skills over and over again to make the perfect shot.

This drive for perfection is what enhances humanity, it drives us forward. However, driving for absolute perfection can also have an adverse effect. It can create an obsession that isn't healthy, it can affect our concentration, it can affect how we view the world. We are constantly looking for perfection in everything, the thing is we will never achieve perfection. In reality there is no such thing as perfection, there is always something that could have been done better even by a tiny tiny little bit. So it's a chase towards the impossible. That doesn't mean not to improve and drive forward, it means drive forward, set the goals, but make them realistic. Push the boundaries but be aware that you are pushing the boundaries and you may not achieve your high and lofty goals. Nothing is perfect and that's the whole point in life, if everything was perfect life would be boring, people would be boring. We need to set realistic goals and we will achieve realistic results. We won't be so consumed by an expectation that is not real, we won't be blinded by the future and will appreciate what we have. Drive for improvement, aim for the best, strive and drive forward just don't aim for the perfect outcome. Things will change and shift and that's the fun in life. Aim high and let the goals shift as you enjoy the journey to your goals.

Part of life is being flexible and adapting to change, the result can change, the destination can change. Appreciate the journey towards improvement, take it all in, absorb it, appreciate it, just don't expect the 100% perfect result as it will never be achieved. Some may read this and say "hey this guy has quit out, he's not aiming for the best". I say, aim for your best, just don't expect perfection, one person's view on perfection is also not the same as another's. We all have different perspectives on life. If you are looking for perfection then you will be disappointed. Life's variety lies in the imperfections, the wrinkles on someone's face tell their lives story, the crumbling of old brick walls tell us that the building has stood the test of time, the brush strokes in a work of art contain the spirit of the artist. The bumps in the road are what build us and define us. If everything in life was perfect then we would drudge along in some kind of Truman Show real life movie. Pretending that things need to be perfect, they don't and that's where the inspiration in life lies. Don't look for the perfect partner, they don't exist, sure they can tick a lot of boxes but that fairytale, whilst you may get close you will never achieve it, and that's a good thing. If we set ourselves up for perfection and only want perfection we miss out on all the quirks of life, we miss out on experiences, we miss out on time with people. If you have kids and expect them to all be harmonious together and get straight A's, being kind and changing the world on a daily basis, you are just going to be disappointed and set your children to fail in your eyes. If you're looking for the perfect partner, who meets everyone of your needs, treats you like the perfect prince or princess and hangs off your every word, that will be boring and you will not be happy. Looking for perfection will stop you finding that partner as you will rule out great candidates, it will make you find flaws in people where there aren't really flaws to be found, it will make you not forgive someone when they should be forgiven. It will set you up for a life of high expectations that you won't achieve.

Instead strive and drive for the best, but see what is around you and appreciate the imperfections in life. The ups and downs are what define us. It's the ebb and flow of life that allows us to learn and grow, things aren't perfect and that is totally fine. In fact it's more than fine, it's exactly what I expected. You will lead a much happier life. That doesn't say to not have dreams, have dreams, just ride the journey along the way. Have high expectations, just don't have them for perfection as you will be forever chasing an unrealistic dream. I have an approach that might not be for everyone, 80% is good enough in everyday cases. Okay, okay, no one wants

80% is good enough when you are going in for brain surgery, let's be honest we kind of expect a 99.9% chance. However, in most everyday situations in life, and I stress everyday situations, 80% is generally good enough. Something is 80% correct then it's usually good enough to satisfy the requirement. If you're constantly looking for 100% you may be there forever and take far more time than needed or never achieve your goal. 80% though that is achievable. It meets most of the requirements, but maybe not all, and in most, again everyday occasions, that is fine. When it's life or death and there are serious consequences then yes I accept we strive for much higher success or completion rate, never 100% though as that's perfection, which doesn't really exist. If your work is 80% correct then that's good, 80% on a test is good enough for most, 80% of the food shopping was done, that's fine. It doesn't mean slack off, it just means that you can achieve 80% of what you were looking for and then move on. You did a great job. Aim high but remember nothing is perfect.

Zenquest:

Is there an area of your life in which you are looking for perfection? Have you ever achieved perfection? Is 80%

good enough for what you are looking to achieve?

Zenbite:

Drive for greatness but not perfection.

Chapter 13: Dark and light

The dark

The world around us is shaped by light and dark. In its most simple distinction 24 hours is split between day and night and therefore light and dark. Many people are afraid of the dark, but no one is afraid of the light. Why is that? The dark is mysterious, you can't see all the detail, things are hidden, things are hiding, you're not sure what lurks there, and in many ways it feels cold. On the flip side in the light we can see, everything is bright and lit up, it's warm, it's inviting. However, don't fear the dark. The dark can be wonderful and contain amazing things. In the context of the physical world the night holds the stars, amazing animals come out at night, insects thrive in the night and wondrous colours and lights can emerge from the natural world. Don't fear the dark. In the context of the mind, things can lurk in the darkness. Things we don't want to touch or experience. Things that have been buried away that we don't want to shine the light on. However, they are there, they are part of us. If we fear them they just grow and grow. Staying away from them allows the fear to grow and the unknown to grow. The fear in our mind grows in ways we don't even know is happening. It's in our subconscious working away, analysing things, over thinking things, comparing things. Referencing things in our past, maybe dark things, that affect and influence our daily lives all without us even knowing or being aware of them. They can alter our perception of a situation or other people. In the dark things can grow stronger.

However, if we embrace the dark and not fear it we can shed light on things. In the nighttime garden the darkness is there, who knows what is present, what creatures lie there waiting for us, but if we turn on a torch we can see things. Once we shine a light on those things that we feared it may be fine. Either way if we don't shine the light we'll never know what is lurking there and our mind will create a whole range of experiences and situations. If we turn on the light and things turn out to be OK then it's all good, we had nothing to worry about. If things aren't quite what we expected then we can embrace and look to resolve them. Without shining a light we will never know. In the mind if we close things off into the dark they can fester. We need to shine the light on the dark parts of the mind to explore and discover what's in there. It may not be pretty, but it's there. It's always going to be there unless we shine the light on it. Take a look, explore, process and realise, with time, and help, that the darkness isn't as bad as we thought.

Once we embrace the dark we can start to process it and in time turn the dark into light. If there is something from your past that is in the shadows of your memories then it may be affecting your daily life. Lingering there in the past, why do you have an aversion to a certain person, place or activity. Is there something in your past, hidden away in the dark that you are not aware of. If we process it we can start to learn and heal, we can shed light on it and begin the journey of moving forward. The dark is there to guide us, to teach us and for us to learn. We just need to embrace it and not fear it.

The light

The light brings everything into focus and can transform how we see things. Those dark days can be turned into brilliant light by focusing on the positive side of things. This doesn't mean walking around in a blissful and ignorant state ignoring all the things happening around in the world, but it means to focus on the good. Sometimes it's easier to focus on the dark and get trapped in it. The dark, in a strange way, can sometimes feel comforting. When we go to sleep it's dark, we wrap ourselves up in a duvet or blanket, getting all snug, we turn off the light and we enter the darkness to go to sleep and rest. Sometimes sitting and staying in the dark can be easier, we don't have to face things, we can stay inside physically and mentally. It's dark, no one is here, I can't see anyone, I don't need to face anyone. Bad things have happened to me, I'm justified that I'm staying in the dark. The world is harsh and I'm better off staying here. I have a reason to stay in the dark, it's justified. Embrace the dark to process it but don't get stuck there. Focus on the light, the positive things happening around you in the world. Things can range from small to large. For example you have a daily commute, it's not great but it's something that is required to get to your work, reframe your mindset to be that the commute gives you time to yourself, time to think, time to do something that you enjoy that you don't usually have time to do. There is something positive to be taken from every situation, whether it be a positive or negative event. There is always something to learn to expand your knowledge. This applies even to those negative things that happen in your life, process them, take them on board and see the learnings you can take away with you.

Through this process focusing on the light can allow you to focus on the positive in every situation. This will lift your mood, mindset and approach to life and your days. The rain brings dreary days, it also brings life to the plants. The sun brings hot, uncomfortable days but it also works with water to bring life. Everything works in balance, the positive and negative, the light and the dark. Don't let the dark overcome you. Focus on the light in life and the positivity it can bring.

Life will feel much lighter, freer, engaging, rewarding if we focus on the light that is provided each day. It's there in front of us, we just need to see it. This will be easier for some more than others. Some, due to life experiences, mindset or genetics can find it hard to see the light in things. They have a dark veil over their eyes which prevents them from seeing the light. If you know someone like this, help them see the light, spend time with them, listen to them, encourage them to share. Sharing a burden can help lighten the load and shift someone's mindset. Setting them free from the burdens they are carrying. Help them lighten that load and let them see the light peaking through the clouds. Dark and tough times will come, they just will, embrace them, process them, work through them, but see the light in life. It will grow, it will allow you to manifest your dreams, it will help you process trauma, it will help you move on, it will help you see the good in those around and the world around you. Light is the path forward in life, to chase your dreams, feel comfort in your surroundings and be yourself. Bathe yourself in your life and the light that is in your world. Channel the inner light within you, the light that shines bright in the shadows even when the days are dark. The spark that comes from your inner being, your imagination, your dreams, your positivity. Bring it all to the surface and embrace the light, let your inner light shine from within and show the world your inner light. It doesn't have to be a grand gesture but showing your inner light to others can lighten their day. Shine your light. Embrace the light that shines from others in your life, you may know that person you may not but embrace the light that you encounter in your interactions with others. It could be someone on the street that is walking with a smile on their face, it could be a small gesture by a stranger, it could be a big gesture by a close friend.

Embrace the light that others shine into the world. Sometimes there are situations and people that just make you smile, they give out a positivity and brightness that brings joy to your day. Absorb this light and take it with you into your day. You can then pass it onto others to bring light to the world.

Zenquest:

Think of all the things in life that bring you joy and light. Think of the positive things around you each day. Really feel them, how does it affect your mood?

Zenbite:

Embrace the dark and bring it into the light. See all the positive light around you each day.

ACTION

Chapter 14: Simple and small

L ife is complicated, lots of decisions to be made, lots of things to do, lots of people to see. Whilst life contains lots of complications and big changes, it can be simplified down a lot. Put simply life is made up of lots of simple decisions. OK, what does that mean? Let me explain, think of a decision as Yes or No. Whilst a decision can have huge consequences and feel complex the decision itself is often a choice between A or B or Yes or No.. Some examples include, shall we get married: yes or no, shall we have kids; yes or no, shall I accept this job; yes or no, shall we have burgers for dinner; yes or no. Whilst this may seem over simplistic, every decision no matter how complex is nearly all of the time a yes or no decision. Even the most complicated question can be boiled down to a yes or no decision, now it may form a series of yes or no decisions but each step on the way is a yes or no decision. Take this example, shall we buy a house; yes, do we want 3 bedrooms, no, do we want 4 bedrooms, yes. Do we want it in this neighbourhood; yes. Do we want a pool, yes. Does it need a garage, yes. And so on.

Simple and small

You see distilling down a question to its core and bare components simplifies the decision. The key part here is that once a decision has been simplified to its core, then it makes it far easier for your intuition to kick in. Having a complex decision with lots of outcomes can feel like brain fog. Distil it down. Keep it simple.

Importantly, just because a decision is simple doesn't mean it can't have far reaching consequences, for example "shall we have kids?" This is a decision that will impact many lives, more lives than you can probably imagine. If you think of the impact of such a decision through time, the repercussions are huge. You decide to have a child, the child before they are born impacts the parents lives. Money needs to be spent on equipment and clothes, family supports the parents and the child, others become aunties and uncles, parents become grandparents and take on a whole new level of responsibility, the child grows up and makes friends, they impact those friends with their words and actions, maybe they are kind or maybe they are unkind. Eventually they decide to go to university, they are accepted, that acceptance into their chosen course may prevent another person from getting into university, and therefore impacting the trajectory of the another person's life, the child gets a job on completion of university, again they get the job instead of someone else, trajectory altered, the child takes a gap year, travels the world, meets new people, impacts their lives, eventually settling down with a partner, trajectory changed and has a child of their own. All of these changes and consequences are widespread, but they all started with that simple decision to have a child, yes or no.

This may all seem overwhelming and complex but the beauty is that life is made up of all of these simple decisions, it doesn't mean they don't need consideration or evaluation but ultimately a decision will be made and it will be in nearly all cases a simple yes or no decision. This simplifies the mind, it simplifies the process, it simplifies everything and therefore allows your intuition to take over. The gut feeling that sits within us has a much easier path to surface itself if the question we are asking is a simple yes or no decision. This can be applied to all parts of your life, when you come to a decision which feels complex, feel into it, what is the yes or no decision that is really happening. Can you step through the questions with more simple yes or no decisions that will help you get to the core of the problem and the solution. Too often we overly complicate decisions and over think them, we introduce way too many variables and factors, which then make the decision much harder to make. Keep any inputs in mind, process them but when it actually comes down to making the decision it can be simplified down to a simple decision. The world is full of people who either over complicate things or those that simplify things. Those that over complicate things can create chaos as they go about their day, they over analyse and create a storm over the simplest of decisions, they involve too many people and too many opinions. They think they are helping but really they are creating noise that makes the decision or event more complicated than it actually is. You will know people like this in your life, they make things feel hard, nothing is straightforward, every decision seems like they are flying to the moon. Maybe you're one of these people, you over think and cause chaos and stress in your own mind and those around you. A storm seems to follow you or things seem to take forever to be decided. On the flip side, the world also contains those who simplify things. They get all the inputs and distill them down to simple information or simple decisions. Whilst it's great to involve others and analyse the information, if you want to move forward those that simplify the process can move everyone forward. They bring calm to the chaos, they have a level head and don't get too emotional over the decision, they provide clarity and simplification to their day and decisions. Look for the simplification in life.

Life is full of big moments, things that shift the fundamentals of your life. Getting married, having kids, moving away from home, choosing a college or university to attend, changing jobs. All these moments are clear sliding door moments, you can appreciate the impact of these decisions and the moments before, during and after they happen. Lots of thought usually goes into these decisions as you know the impact they will have on your life. Time is spent deciding, others are questioned for their advice, the process could be short or long but the magnitude is generally recognised. These decisions will have an impact on your life, a clear measurable impact on how your life will flow. These decisions are visible, clear and measurable. We see them in front of our eyes. Just as important, maybe even more important, are the small decisions that impact your life. Those seemingly insignificant moments, the quick decision, the change of mind that all appear to be small and hey it doesn't matter. These decisions can swing your life and significantly change the course of your life. They are classic sliding door moments too. In fact the small decisions in life are what actually shape us as people, and the impact we have on those around us. They are decisions that we are more likely to make without thinking, on a whim and essentially tapping into our intuition. These are the small decisions that we are confident to make on our own, we don't ask others opinions, we are more likely to just go ahead with the decision. Sure, some of these decisions will be small and have no impact upon our lives other than what we intended from those decisions, shall I eat this apple, not much impact upon our lives. Other decisions though will send us on a trajectory that at the time will be totally unknown to us. Say for example, you decide attend a concert on your own, it's a simple decision, maybe you've never been on your own before but intuition drives you to the concert, at the concert you meet the person of your dreams, or maybe you get inspired by the bass guitarist to join a band or you discover a new favourite song that motivates you to change something in your life. The point is deciding to go to the concert was a small decision that impacted your life in a way that allows you to discover something you love. Now, I don't want you thinking "hey this guy said that small decisions are important, so I better consider all decisions before I make them." Life would be too hard if we ran our lives like this. The point is, run with those small decisions, let them flow through your life, continue to make them, embrace them, do them based off of your gut as they will be driven by your intuition and take you places that you never dreamed.

This doesn't mean simple and small decisions don't have colour and are simply black and white, they are simple, small and maybe plain but they build up and add colour. Take a grain of sand on its own. It's just a small grain of sand, yellow or white in colour, now multiply it by millions and it becomes an amazing beach. Look closely at an oil painting, it's made up of small brush strokes, individually they are small one colour strokes but zoom out and you see the full glory of the artwork. Everything can start from something simple and small to grow into something much larger. Take computer code, it's just 1s and 0s, individually they are nothing but combine them together and you get amazing software, images and apps. All starting from a small seemingly insignificant object. Just because a decision or object is simple or small doesn't mean it doesn't have colour and feeling.

Let those simple and small decisions into your life. Your intuition says, turn left. Small decision, do it. The voice in your head says go for that run, small decision, do it. Your mind says go down a new path that you've never been down before, small decision, do it. Embrace the flow, embrace your mind driving your body as you never know where life will take you.

Zenquest:

Think of a big decision you have made, was it a simple yes or no decision? Do you have a big decision currently in your life, can you distill it down to yes or no?

Zenbite:

Life's decisions can be simplified, helping us follow our intuition. Small decisions can have a great impact upon our lives and allow our intuition to come through.

Chapter 15: Purpose

T hroughout our lives our purpose can shift and change, for many when we are young our purpose is to have fun, socialise with friends, play games and enjoy life. We want to experience life and that is our purpose. The vast majority of children focus on enjoyment in life, that is their purpose and that's the way it should be. When we are young we have no worries, things are done for us, our parents look after us and we simply enjoy what life has to offer and look to learn. Digging in the sand, running through fields, riding a bike, swimming in the ocean. At this point I appreciate that not all children have this luxury and for some their early years can be hard, I'm not disregarding those kids. They have it tough. As kids though we come into the world for enjoyment and fun, even if times are tough, we look for the light and enjoyment in life. As adults we should encourage this phase. As we get older things shift a little, we go to school and things can become more focused. Our purpose at this stage is to begin our learning journey and to develop our skills whether they be physical or more creative. On the social side we begin to make friends and learn how to interact with others. Our purpose is to learn skills that will serve us during our childhood and in later life. As we age further our purpose begins to become more complex as we enter the teenage years. Things start to get a little complicated now, hormones develop, our minds and bodies start to develop as we start to change. Our purpose at this stage is to see where we fit in the world and start to map out our future. This is different for everyone and can be a challenging time. We are still growing and rapidly learning and evolving. Our purpose is to begin the journey of being more independent. As we move into adulthood we start thinking about careers, partners, owning a home, travelling, having children, getting married and our purpose can shift greatly. We may even have multiple purposes such as raising a family, running our own business, being an employee at work, looking after family members, supporting the community. When we enter adulthood we can take on lots of different responsibilities, each coming with their own direction and purpose. Some of these will be challenging and some will be fun. It's part of life to evolve and grow. Having a purpose throughout our life and its stages gives us direction and fulfilment. Without purpose or a feeling of purpose we can begin to feel lost.

A purpose doesn't have to be a grand gesture, such as

saving the planet. In our own way we contribute to society and those around us. A purpose can be looking after elderly parents, taking care of children, helping people connect with each other, being a bus driver and providing a way for people to get to work. A purpose can be anything. Having a purpose gives us guidance and fulfilment, it gives us a place in the world. It can vary greatly from person to person, and it varies throughout our lives but that feeling or having a purpose is valuable to our wellbeing. It gives us a sense of wellbeing and meaning. To be honest, we may not always agree with our purpose. A housewife / househusband whose purpose it is to run the household may not agree or like their purpose but it is a purpose. The first step is finding purpose in your life, you may like it or you may not but just having any purpose provides direction and is better than not having any purpose. Some people may thrive in being the housewife or house husband role, whilst others may not like it. It's about having a purpose in life as it gives you direction, something to aim at. Having no direction is counter productive to moving forward, doing nothing results in, well nothing. We lose our drive and start to question why we are here. I don't have any purpose, good or bad, I am just existing in what seems a meaningless life. The second key is finding a purpose that resonates with you. This is when you really thrive and take your life to the next level, you are operating in life with a purpose that brings you joy. Ideally one that makes your heart sing and gets you up and about everyday with enthusiasm. This is when we really bring joy to the world and those around us. We are contributing to our world and it feels good.

A life without purpose can feel dark, lost, confusing. What am I doing today? I have no purpose. A day or life without purpose can make us feel lost, we feel empty, unsure of what we are contributing. We can have mixed emotions, we're confused as to what our place is and why we are here. What is my purpose? On a day to day level we can drill down to having a purpose for that day. It may be something complex, I am running an important meeting at work or something simple, I'm doing the weekly grocery shop. Either way we have a purpose to the day, when we complete what we set out to achieve we feel good. We feel we have achieved something, big or small, complex or simple. Having a purpose or multiple purposes will drive us forward and allow us to feel achievement when we complete goals that align with our purpose. If that is missing you can feel lost with no direction. On the scale of things, ideally we want to have a purpose that feels good and fills our heart. If that's currently not happening it's good to just have a purpose that gives you some direction and feedback for your day and actions. Without a feeling of direction we can feel lost. Feeling lost is not a great feeling. Feeling physically lost, where am I? Is not a great feeling. Feeling mentally lost is even worse. What am I doing? That weighs down on your mind and therefore your body. It weighs you down and those around you. Find a simple purpose, expand on that to find a purpose that brings you joy. Keep it simple at first and then expand as you grow and start to gain confidence.

Importantly it needs to be your purpose, not someone else's. If you lead a life that is driven by others then you will feel unfulfilled and it will create resentment within you. To truly have a life that is filled with purpose it needs to be your own goals and drive. Otherwise you are just living someone else's life. That's not what you want. Find a purpose that feels true to you, use your intuition, what feels right, what feels wrong. Your intuition will guide you towards your true purpose. You may not have everything clear in your mind and know exactly what your purpose is, this is fine and totally normal. You just need to start heading in the direction you think is best, go with your intuition with a feeling of purpose and fulfilment. If you go with the flow, then life will guide you down the right path. Your fulfilment will grow and if you keep doing what is true to you and listening to your intuition then your feeling of purpose will grow. This will allow you to lead a fulfilled life that is true to you. You will have purpose and a purpose that is yours.

Zenquest:

Write down your current purpose in life. Do you feel like you have one at all? If this isn't obvious, take a look at the different areas of your life, family, work, friends.

When you find your purpose or purposes. Are they fulfilling you? If not, how can you adapt your daily life for more fulfilment, how can you give your life a meaningful purpose that resonates with you. Changes in this area could be big or small depending upon your circumstances.

Zenbite:

Don't underestimate the power of having a purpose in life. Something that gives you direction, a feeling of fulfilment and achievement.

Chapter 16: Fun

O ne of my favourite things. Simply having fun. I don't think anyone can underestimate the importance of having fun. Fun can come in many forms for people. It could be playing sports, going out for dinner with friends, going for a run, playing with the kids, taking in a movie, walking on the beach, playing the saxophone, the list is literally endless. Taking time out to have fun is a core part of life. It relates to having balance, if all you do is work (especially work that you don't enjoy) and no fun, then the world can be a dull and serious place. Don't forget work itself can be fun if you're in your dream job. Just because it's work doesn't mean it has to be boring. It's often said that those that find joy in their work never work a day in their lives, therefore the line between work and fun is blurred. I think this is one of life's goals, the ability to find fun, enjoyment and enrichment in all areas of your life. Unfortunately not many in the world achieve this goal, and I do have to concede that it's not always possible right away, sometimes we may need to work and not enjoy it. I'm not being a downer, just realistic. Whilst everyone should have this goal and staying in an unfulfilling job shouldn't be a goal, there will be times when you may find yourself in a situation where work is just not fun. Even though you try it's just the way it is. What you can do is start to take the steps to alleviate this, learn new skills, switch jobs, and have fun outside of work. Look for ways in your life to have fun outside of work, whilst you work on the goal of finding fun in your work. Don't accept the long term goal that work shouldn't be fun. It should be, it just may take time to find the right fit but it is possible. Fun is the lightness in life, without fun life would feel hard and heavy.

How do we achieve fun? Good question, fun will come in many forms for different people. It goes back to looking at you. It generally always does and sounds like I'm always going on about you, you, you, but it really is about you. Look at the ways in which fun enriches your life today. What are the fun things that you like to do? It could be cooking, exercise, seeing friends, spending time alone, spending time with family. Finding what brings life and enrichment will unlock the fun in your days. Look inside and see what makes you shine. List out the things that you find fun, try to incorporate these into your day before, during or after work. If work isn't fun, start to incorporate the fun outside of work. Once you've mastered fun outside of work, look at how you can bring fun to your work day. It could be having coffee with a colleague, going for a run at lunch time, arranging work events to lighten the mood. Work is often, work, work, work and can become a drag. Insert activities whether they be physical or mental (yoga or pilates at lunch) into your day. I do believe once you've mastered fun outside of work, and bring touches of fun into your work day, the days will start to feel lighter and easier. However, don't rest on this. Look at your work, your goals. What is it in your work that would bring fun to those days. It could be in the same job or company or it could be something completely different. Start to make steps to bring this change, even just the action of starting to make some changes will make you feel better and enhance your days. You can see light, even if it's dim, at the end of the tunnel.

Put simply, find the fun in life. Life is there to be lived, not drudged through every day. I've been there and done that. I don't mince my words in that it can feel awful. Long work days that drag on forever with no fun or enjoyment insight. The world feels dark, boring, hard, pretty much any negative word you can think of.

But bringing fun into your life can start to transform your days, it brings in the light and laughter. Seriously, laughter is amazing. Find me someone who doesn't like to laugh! It relaxes your mind, frees it up from any worries, you can feel any problems lighten even just for a few minutes. This spreads to your body, you can feel the negative energy pour out of your body, your face feels light, your whole body feels light. Find those people around you that make you feel good, who lighten your day and bring a smile to your face. We all need those people in our life. They aren't always loud, outgoing people. It's those people in your life that bring a smile to your face, make you laugh and give you that good feeling and you feel good being around them. You need those people in your life. If you have those people in your life already, cherish them, spend time with them, make sure you arrange to spend time with them. If you don't have those people in your life then look to start something new, join a group, reconnect with old friends who did bring you joy, go with a fun open mindset and those with a similar mindset will connect with you.

It can sometimes feel hard to find the fun in life. Things can get tough, but you don't need to feel that way. Just as you can find nature all around you, you can start to look for the fun and enjoyment in your life and those around you. Don't take life so seriously, at the end we all die (dramatic tone), but it's true. If we go through life not looking for joy and fun then life is serious. A serious life isn't a good life. It could be a productive one in terms of financial wealth but really is that wealth. I don't think so. Wealth comes from the fun and positivity in life. It comes from the lighter moments in life. Sure the darker moments will mould you, they will allow you to grow and they gave us valuable experience but we don't want to stay that way. Take the learnings from the dark moments and use them to drive you forward towards the light, towards the fun and playfulness within life. Children want to have fun. Adults who want to have fun are often looked down upon. Get serious. Be serious. Sometimes people may say "you're a grown up you can't go through life having fun" or "you need to grow up." I don't think anything could be further from the truth. Having fun is a part of life, it's a right, it's a privilege, everyone of any age could and should be having fun. Whether it's doing something on your own or an activity with others you need to have fun in your life. For those that frown upon fun they are frowning upon life, they aren't leading a fulfilled life, in fact they are passing on their disappointments and negativity to others. Everyone deep down is just a little boy and girl, we may be older and wiser but we are that same person from many years ago. The little boy who would run through the fields laughing, the little girl who would play with her friends in the playground, the little boy who loved to play football (soccer) or the little girl who played the violin. Having fun is not a bad thing, it's finding enjoyment in all areas of life, it's connecting back to the spirit of when we were young with no cares in the world. It's finding joy in the things that we love and with the people that we love. It brings a smile to our faces and we should embrace fun at every step, we should look for and encourage fun. I get it that there are sometimes serious times, from being in an exam, job interview, a funeral but they are just passing moments. Sure you need to be serious from time to time in certain situations, but in those everyday moments, those moments where fun is right in front of you, grab it! In those situations if someone puts a downer on you for having fun, talk to them, see if they want to join in, find out what they don't want to have fun, but keep going with life and enjoying the fun it brings.

Seriousness has its place but it shouldn't be the dominating mood throughout your life. See the lighter side, embrace the fun and take the opportunities in front of you to have fun. They won't always come but when they do you grab them and keep hold for the ride. No one ever wanted to be more boring on their deathbed. Cherish your family and friends, they are the ones that know you best and bring light into your life. They are there for the good and bad times. Ride out the bad times and embrace the good times. Dance, laugh, joke and bring joy to yourself and those around you. Life is there to be lived. Embrace the fun.

Zenquest:

Make a list of things that you find fun. You may be doing them now, you may not. Either way include them in your list. Now take a look at whether you're actually those things. How can you incorporate these things into your day?

Think of those people in your life that make you smile and laugh, how often do you see them, can you see them more? Bring them into your life to bring joy to both of you.

Zenbite:

Have fun and don't take life seriously.

Chapter 17: The power of no

In life many occasions arise in which we are asked to do something for someone else, whether we are asked to help a friend, complete a specific task at work or fulfil a task that is expected of our role in life, whether that be as a parent, family member or employee. The list is endless of things we may be asked to complete during a normal day. Most people's tendency to such requests is to say yes, in particular within work, family or friend environments. We feel an obligation to complete the task, it's our role, it's our duty, we must complete the task as we've been asked. It's expected of us. Have you ever been asked to do a task in work knowing that it will take you a long time, maybe hours to complete and really it's a task that shouldn't be asked of you and you shouldn't be even considering doing, but you say yes. Have you ever been asked by a friend to help, but it will require you to rearrange your whole schedule for the day, stop you from doing something you love, cause an inconvenience, but regardless you say yes. Sometimes in life we do need to suck it up, see the bigger picture, take one on the chin and help others out even if it inconveniences us. However, sometimes when the importance of the task isn't great and the impact isn't too large we can simply say no. However, we find no the hardest word to say, it's much easier to just say yes and get on with it.

Children appear to find it quite easy to say no, tidy your room, no. Eat your vegetables, no. Take out the rubbish, no. They have a sense of independence in themselves, I don't want to do that task, I would rather be playing outside. They often have the confidence to simply say no to our requests. I understand this will vary per family and situation but overall children have the confidence to simply say no when a task is presented to them that doesn't meet their needs. However, as we progress into adulthood many of us seem to lose this ability to say no. As a child we say no I don't like that, I don't want to do that. This ability and respect for our own needs seems to fade away when we enter adulthood. Why is that?

Put simply, quite often saying no is much harder than saying yes. Yes is easy, you say yes and everyone is happy. The other person gets their needs fulfilled and they are happy, and in some instances that could be enough to make you happy. Sometimes though it results in everyone else being happy, everyone else except you. Inside your screaming no, no, no but you say yes. It's easier just to do what is asked of you, not to upset anyone, to toe the line and be part of the team. It feels easier and saves a lot of negotiation and potential emotional trauma that we feel will come from the situation if we say no. We feel a need to please others, we are part of the group, we don't want to be left out of the group, we want to be helpful and kind so we put others first. Maybe there's some deep seated need from hunter gatherer times when we needed the safety of the pack or maybe it's our ego just wanting to be liked and not upset others. Whilst this is OK on occasion, it's those occasions when we really don't have the time, skills or motivation and we really should be saying no, but it's easier to say yes. Don't get me wrong, sometimes we should help others, but if you continually do so at the constant detriment to yourself this will take a toll on your mind and sense of wellbeing. You may start to feel powerless or taken advantage of. Your friendship, family or work life could take a turn for the worse, you start to view others in a negative light but now you've got yourself in this situation and have set an expectation and now there is no way out unless you upset the other person. To extract yourself out of the situation may require skill and effort, and you think it's just not worth it. Sometimes though we need to put ourselves first and look after ourselves. In the long run, constantly helping others and saying yes with a negative impact upon ourselves will have a negative effect on our life. Yes is sometimes easier, but it doesn't mean it's the right answer.

No is a powerful statement when used in the correct way. If it's something minor and you're just being awkward or lazy then no probably isn't the correct answer, it will vary per situation. Deep down you know your answer is no, and you stray away from your inner intuition it will eat at you inside. Why did I say yes, I should have said no and now I'm feeling the impact. Saying no is standing up for yourself, it can be putting yourself or your family first. Sometimes we all need to say no. No is sometimes how change happens, standing up for yourself and those around you. Saying no when it's the right answer. There is real power in saying no. It's much more powerful than saying yes. No means you are taking a stance, standing up for your needs or rights. You are putting your views first. It's much harder to say no, but by doing so you are showing courage. Those that say you are not being part of the team or being selfish are being selfish themselves. They are imposing their actions or needs onto you without owning it themselves. Again, this doesn't apply if we know we are just being awkward or lazy. We need to feel it in our bones, my answer is no and I stand by it. Stand your ground for what you believe in.

Saying no can simply be a request from a friend to go out for the night, when you really know you need study for collage, it can be saying no to your boss at work when you are being asked an unreasonable request, to standing up for yourself and making a political statement and saying no to those in power who are abusing that power. Saying no takes the power away from those that are abusing it, whether this be in government or within your friend or family circle. Stand up for yourself and have the courage to say no. A personal example of this was my son who was 6 years old at the time. As a family we planned a trip to the cinema with his sisters to watch the Barbie movie. He really didn't want to go, like really didn't want to go. It wasn't that he was being lazy or awkward; he genuinely didn't want to go. Polite negotiations started which slowly escalated in an attempt to get him to go to the movies. Due to his age, if he wasn't to go then I wouldn't be able to go and our family trip would no longer be a full family trip. He stood his ground, the anger and annoyance grew on both sides. Until, it went so far that I switched from being annoyed with him to having respect for him. He was standing his ground, his answer was no, a real solid no and he was sticking to it no matter what. Fair enough I thought, eventually, he's standing up for himself and I need to respect that. Even though it had consequences to me I could see that to force him to go would be forcing him to go against his will. Whilst it was only a minor event, it showed him that he had the courage to say no and that I respected him enough to value his decision. I'm not saying it was a straightforward interaction, but in the end we ended up with respect for each other. He had the power to say no.

Zenquest:

Think of a time when you've said yes when really you should have said no. How did it make you feel? What was the outcome, did it negatively impact you? If you had said no, what would have been the consequences?

Zenbite:

Yes is easy, sometimes the power lies in saying no

Chapter 18: Positive and negative

Everyone makes mistakes, whether they are a big humdinger or small and seemingly insignificant, everyone makes them all the time. Mistakes are just part of life. No one is perfect after all, and why should we be perfect? If we were how boring life would be, everyone walking around in their perfect lives doing their perfect things. Boring. Mistakes are part of life and it's something we need to accept. The sooner we accept this then the better we can view our mistakes and learn from them. Mistakes define us, they are what mould us into who we are. Whilst we can learn from the things we execute perfectly, that feeling of making a good meal, the perfect goal in a soccer game, completing level 53 on candy crush or nailing a job interview. We learn from these events and experiences, they give us the validation of what works. We did something this way and it worked, awesome, so next time this is what I need to do to repeat the success. We learn from positive experiences, they expand our knowledge on what works for us. They guide us towards future success.

However it is the mistakes that define us.

Making a mistake often feels bad, we feel bad for ourselves, we feel bad for others. I made a mistake. I'm so sorry. But. What if we see mistakes as positive? Something that we can grow from. That doesn't mean we walk around trying to mess things up all the time so that we can try to learn from them, but instead we can look at our experience and think about what we can learn. You messed up, accept it, move on but make sure you take the learnings with you. Whether an experience or outcome was positive or negative there is always something to take away. Mistakes are a learning experience, we find out something about ourselves or others and the best form of action to take. I say that's a win. We do something positive, we learn something new, win. We do something negative, we learn something new, win. Strive for the result you want, but if things don't go your way then it just wasn't meant to be. Think about what you can learn from this experience, how you can do things differently next time. Positive experiences and outcomes can sometimes make us complacent, we succeed so we don't need to grow, we achieved what we set out to complete, we nailed it, learning done. We don't want to get into this trap from positive experiences, we want to learn and grow from positive experiences. Negative experiences though give us that jolt, oh that didn't go as planned, learn from it. The negative thoughts give you a shove. They can jolt us too much sometimes, I don't want to do that again I didn't like it. Sometimes you find your boundaries and that's fine, you learnt something new, you learnt where your true boundaries lie. Other times you need to take that learning and use it to help you learn and grow. Mistakes may freak us out or upset us, but deep down we know whether we want to pursue something or not. If you fail, and deep down you know that thing is just not for you then that's fine, you learnt something new about yourself. However, if deep down you know you can do it, this is what you dreamed of, take the negative experience, learn from it and make it a positive.

Every experience is positive whether it's successful or not, if we view our actions in this way it means we can tackle every experience, whether new or old with some level of confidence. If this goes well, great I succeeded. I can learn from this even more for next time. If I mess up, great what can I learn from this experience. It's not always easy to do, especially when it involves others. There's nothing worse than messing up in front of others, you feel embarrassed, you feel bad. Grab that feeling and see what you can learn from it. Why do you feel that way? What can you take away from that experience? Maybe you just learnt your limits, that's fine, maybe this activity isn't the one for you, but you learnt something new about yourself. It's better to try and fail, than not to try at all. Take something positive from the experience. In this way, whatever we do, we take something positive from it. Turn the negative into a positive, thus allowing us to walk through life with more grace and confidence. It doesn't matter what happens I will learn and grow from it either way.

Thinking this way can give us much more confidence within a situation and it can be a powerful mind shift. Instead of shying away from a new experience or activity, we can dive straight in. Sure we'll still have those nerves, which is totally fine, but we will take that step forward knowing that it may be a little scary but either way come success or failure we will learn something new, something positive can be taken from the experience. It's quite a big shift to make in your mindset but it is a powerful change that will open you up to new experiences and give you a new found sense of confidence.

Zenquest:

Think of a time you messed up and things didn't go to plan. Did you learn from that experience? If not, could you have learnt from the experience? Would that learning give you something positive to take forward with you?

Think of something that feels a little daunting, now think that whatever the outcome you will grow as a person and it will be a positive experience either way. Do you view the upcoming experience in a different way?

Zenbite:

Tackle life regardless of the outcome. There's always something to learn. Go ahead with confidence.

Chapter 19: Don't put things off

O ne trick I learnt many years ago, to have a more relaxed mindset, was to do things now and don't put them off. A classic example in my life was something that needed to be done in work. It was Friday afternoon so I thought I'd leave it and put it off until Monday, but then I would get to Sunday evening and think "ah man I have to do that thing tomorrow at work. I wish I had already done it on Friday." So that's what I started to do, whenever there was something I was putting off and I was in the 'it's Friday afternoon' mindset I would go and do it. I felt so much better for it. When I would head into work on Monday morning, that feeling of dread was no longer there. The task I had put off I had done. Throughout the weekend it never crossed my mind because I had completed the task. I felt relieved. So I applied to other areas of my life. As soon as you get that feeling that you don't want to do something but it's something you need or should do, you know that feeling of dread down in your stomach. That's the time to do it. Don't put it off. If you're not clear in your mind, then sure put it off, you might need to think about it a little longer. Don't rush the action or decision. However, if you know deep down, your intuition knows the correct thing to do, act upon it. All it will do is gnaw away at your mind, it will cloud your judgement, it will make your mind fuzzy, it will put you on edge. The action or decision could be anything. Something big or something small. Sometimes the things that gnaw at us the most are those small things. We don't voice our opinion or follow through with an action. We knew it was the right thing to do but we put it off. We create a level of stress within us, we know what is right for us and we put it off. We may even get a little annoyed with ourselves and frustrated "why didn't I do that?" My advice is just do it.

Doing things now, when they feel right, will clear your mind. Give you clarity. It will create room within your mind and clear your thoughts. Instead of festering away it will create room and a level of clarity and fulfilment that you completed what you wanted to do. You may even feel proud of yourself for doing the action, and you will feel that little bit more proud of yourself for not putting off the action of decision and putting yourself first. You put your mind at rest and now your mind feels better for it. Putting things off just drags them out, often making them bigger things than they were. The action could be anything, switching jobs, telling a friend some bad information, completing a boring task at work, having an awkward conversation with your partner, doing the dishes! It's much better to get things out of the way than let them grow. The energy around the action or decision just grows more negative and gets bigger. The energy could be built within you or the negative energy between you and another person. It will build and build and can sometimes get out of control, starting to consume your mind or build up a wall within your mind or your interaction with another person. You can feel this heaviness within yourself. You feel dragged down, you feel heavy and weighed down by the weight of the action but also weighed down even more through the inaction.

Make the decision, perform the action, have the conversation and the weight will be lifted from your shoulders. You will feel lighter and the other person may feel lighter too. They will likely have picked up on your energy, maybe consciously or unconsciously. Push through the negative energy. Simply performing the action can transform the negative energy into positive energy. The outcome might not be great, someone could get hurt, but the negative energy that has been building has been released, and that's a positive. This can apply to anything large or small. See the positive nature of taking the action and you will feel released. It doesn't always have to be big and complex; it can sometimes be something small and seemingly insignificant, but the small things can add up, especially when there is a lack of action and when action needs to be taken. Small jobs can build up and before you know it you have a long list that feels overwhelming. Don't get overwhelmed, take action when you know you need to take it, don't put it off. Release the energy and you will feel free.

Zenquest:
Think of some things on your to do list, are you being weighed down by not doing them? Why haven't you done them? Do them and notice how you feel afterwards.

Zenbite:
Don't put things off, release the energy and do actions when you know they feel right.

Chapter 20: Experiences

Whilst physical objects and material things can be great and they can bring short term joy to your day and life, quite often if we do get a new material 'toy' it is often the experience of using that 'toy' that gives us joy. Say a teenager gets a new video console, sure it's a new shiny physical product, but what brings the joy is the experience of playing the games and the interaction with friends whether it be online or in person. Getting a new car can feel great but it's the experience and feel of the new car that brings the joy. So even though it's the physical material product that is the trigger or source, it's the resulting experience from that object that is bringing joy, don't dismiss material things as not bringing joy. Whilst the object itself might not bring joy, it's a physical inanimate object, however the experience of using the object can bring joy. Take art for example, you add a new dramatic and emotive art piece to your workspace. Every time you see the art you feel inspired and it drives your creative side to feel better and attain better results, it's a physical object with the enjoyment being driven by the experience of viewing it. There is a relationship between material objects and experiences which I think is sometimes misunderstood, forgotten or misinterpreted. What isn't a good experience driven by material objects is working hard to earn money to buy physical products only for them to be set aside after the novelty has worn off. This is different, this is chasing the dopamine hit of a new product or object and then once you have it, the hit fades and you move onto the next object that you desire. This isn't a fulfilling experience.

Experiences are vital for our lives, whether they are triggered by an emotional event or physical object. Other types of experiences are those that are driven by an event or emotion, not an object. Going for a run, walking along the beach, having a nice meal, sex, holding a newborn baby, watching TV with your kids, laughing and joking with friends at a party. The list of experiences is endless and will vary from person to person. These are the activities we think of when we think of experiences. They are emotional events that we cherish that are driven by our experience with another person or event. Often there is an emotional attachment to the event, whether it be an emotional attachment to the person we are experiencing the event with or simply the event itself. Taking a walk, it's one of life's simplest and most rewarding experiences, whether it be with others or on your own. You are out in the world, breathing in the air, moving your body, it's free, it's simple and everyone can do it as long as you are physically able.

To have a wide range of experiences is to experience life itself.

Experiences build variety in life, they give us insights into ourselves and our thoughts. Without experiences life would be dull and the same monotonous churn every day. Experiences allow us to grow our minds, bodies and our perception of life. They expand our mind to create new reference points, which we can then use to learn even more and have different experiences. Expanding our minds is important for our growth, to feel like we are progressing in life. Without this life can be dull. Experiences bring this to us on a daily basis. It's important to hold space for experiences, observe and absorb what is happening in the event. Doing so will give you an appreciation of what is occurring, how things are affecting you, what you can take away from this experience. Any and every experience will expand your mind in some form.

Experiences are also a key part to take our minds of things, they shift the gears, we learn new things but they can also reset our brains. Take our minds off troubles for a while. This opening, this freedom from our recurring thoughts can allow us to think differently. During our experiences we learn new things, see new things and hear new things which change our thought process and in turn alter our perception of a problem we are experiencing. Thus opening up our minds to new things. Examples of these types of experiences include walking in nature, swimming in the ocean, looking at art. They allow our minds to take us away to another place, to clear our minds, to breathe and enjoy a simple experience. It's just a walk in the local park, but it could be the most important experience you have that day for your mental and physical health. Take the opportunities for these simple yet important experiences. To reset and enjoy the simple things in life. The enjoyment of an experience can release stress and anxiety within our minds and bodies, taking us out of our comfort zone or the daily grind, giving our minds freedom and relaxation. I am a big advocate of having experiences during what is your usual work time, take the day of work, set time aside for yourself to just relax or have a new experience. You are giving yourself this time which enhances the experience even more. You are setting this time aside for yourself, let that sink in, you are looking after yourself and that experience, whether it be an existing or new experience will shift your mind and release stress. Experiences with others can expand the enjoyment even further, a simple meal can be transformed if that meal is with a special person in your life. The experience of just talking to another person can lift your soul, the interaction, the communication, the energy that flows between you. You know when you are in the presence of someone special in your life that you value, you can feel the connection and the enjoyment.

I'm not one to repeat the same experience, holidays in different places, different pubs (I love a good pub crawl), different days out. I like the variety that different places can bring to an experience, seeing new things that you haven't seen before and discovering hidden treasures. I wouldn't call it FOMO but there is a curiosity to see what's around the next corner, to see something new. I know for some this will seem totally off, they like the comfort in visiting the same place. It feels safe, it feels familiar, they know what they like and they've found it. There is nothing wrong with that as people will find comfort in different ways. It's great to have variety but it can also be great to have familiarity. I think this is valuable if you are lucky enough to have kids. If you have a great one off experience as a kid, then, depending upon your age, you will likely remember it. However, not all experiences are once in a lifetime and mind blowing, they're great experiences but if they are one off then sometimes they can get forgotten. This applies to adults, but I think it especially applies to kids. However, if as a child you experienced the same great experience over and over again it creates great memories that go beyond the experience. Going to the same place on holiday once a year, or every few years. Visiting the same water park in the summer on those hot days, visiting family for a Sunday lunch, watching TV on the sofa and eating your favourite meal as a family. The repetition of these experiences can really build fond memories within our minds. When we are older we can look back at these memories with fondness, they make us smile and remind us of certain people, places and feelings. This can be a great gift to your children. It's the one area of my life that I welcome repetition in order to create these latest experiences and fond memories for them. As an adult reminiscing about these memories can really bring a smile to your face, you tell your friends about your memories, they create a safe and warm feeling. You look back at your experiences not just as a great day but as a lasting memory, almost something that defines your personality and outlook on life.

If we're honest not all experiences are going to be positive. We will in life have negative experiences. Things that didn't turn out the way we expected, things that we didn't plan for happened. That's life. Just because an experience is deemed to be negative doesn't mean we can't learn from that experience. Every experience, whether positive or negative, will shape us and allow us to grow. Sometimes the toughest experiences in life are those that shape us. Sure the good times are great, we feel positive and joy fills our lives. When times get tough it's often when the tough questions are asked. You look at yourself, your life and those around you. Even though it may seem hard at the time, negative experiences can allow you to grow even more so than the positive experiences. You learn things about yourself that you never knew. You are tougher than you thought. You grow and experience life in a new way. These experiences mould us as people, they create our personalities and how we view the world. See the positive and negative experiences as opportunities to grow and learn. Experiences can vary from obvious life events, trekking in the Andes, taking a ski trip, learning a new skill. They are all experiences that we can savour and we plan them in our lives, we take out special time in our daily lives to do them, we plan them ahead. We can feel the experience. Also value the small experiences, the everyday things that bring a smile to your face, they bring you a small piece of joy every day if you recognise them. Savour them whether they are big or small, on your own or with others.

Zenquest:
Think of 3 positive and negative experiences and how they have affected your life and way of thinking. Is there something you have been putting off, why not just do it.

Zenbite:
Experiences expand your mind and give back to your soul. Embrace the experiences and opportunities that are presented to you.

Chapter 21: Why not?

O ne of the most profound realisations that I have had over the past few years is embracing the statement "Why not?" When an opportunity is in front of you, whether the universe has brought it to you, if you believe in that kind of thing, or it's simply a set of coincidences, or it's just there in front of you for whatever reason, but you have that pause, that hesitation, simply think to yourself "Why not?" Seriously, just think of those two words, I mean really think of the situation or opportunity, feel it, I mean really feel it and think "Why not?" Should you accept that job promotion, why not? Should you go on that holiday, why not? Should you go on a date with that person, why not? We often put up barriers in front of us for a whole wide range of reasons, they could be past patterns, past behaviours, low confidence, over thinking, the list goes on. We put these barriers in place because we think we are protecting ourselves, whether that be consciously or subconsciously, but we all do it. These barriers that we create can stop us doing things that we want to do, whether they are valid or not, real or not real, we create them. Our mind thinks that it is protecting us, either from spending too much money, having too much fun - because we have a deep seated belief that fun is bad, we aren't skilled enough at something, or others are better than us so it's not worth it, or we simply aren't good enough or deserve it. When these instances arise where there is a decision between our mind and spirit deciding what to do, my advice, as long as the situation is acceptable and you're not breaking the law, or anyone is going to get hurt or you're doing something for all the wrong reasons. You know those legit reasons when you are deciding and it's an honest decision. Think to yourself "Why not?" Why shouldn't you do that activity, adventure, buy that thing? Just because you think why not doesn't mean you're actually going to do it. You may actually come up with a legitimate reason not to, and that's fine. If you want to go for a swim and it's -3c outside with torrential rain and the waves are smashing up the beach, and you think to yourself why not go for a swim? It's probably best to skip that urge, as not all urges will be good ideas.

Those that are good ideas, you know the ones that are deep down, think through why shouldn't you do it?

Why don't you deserve this thing or activity? Will anything bad really happen if you do it, will anyone get hurt, will there be serious consequences from your actions? If not, then why not? Phew, there are a lot of question marks in this chapter. Think about it, feel into it, look at why you're thinking of not doing something, are they real reasons? If there is a genuine reason, then fine, but if your head is full of reasons or excuses that deep down are just excuses, and you'll know they are excuses. You can feel an excuse in your head, it doesn't feel right, it feels off, it feels like a way out, you talk yourself into not doing something. Stop, take a deep breath and really feel into the question you are asking yourself "should I do this experience or opportunity that is presenting itself to me?" If it feels right and your soul is saying yes, but your mind is saying no. Do it. Why not? If it feels right, why not do it? Take the step, make the leap, jump into the unknown. Sure it feels scary but that's what life is about, pushing the boundaries. There is a difference between something not feeling right and your whole body screaming noooo! To something that feels right but you talk yourself out of it. Doing that new drum class, you've always dreamed of it. Joining a group to make new friends, it feels right but you talk yourself out of it. Taking a new job when you're stuck in your current boring and life sucking role. Why not? Why not just do it and see what happens.

If someone asks why you are taking a certain action, buying a new car, taking a new job, taking a new route to work, trying a new restaurant, learning a new skill. If they question why you are doing something, just say "Why not?" In most cases I say they'll be taken aback. Often the person will pause and need to justify the reasons in their own head, they may come up with reasons but are they real reasons or just excuses, and importantly are they their own excuses, not yours. Just responding with "why not?" will often throw them off, they didn't expect that response. Hopefully it will get them thinking about "why not?" Why shouldn't I do this thing that I've always dreamed of. Allow yourself the opportunity to experience something new and something that you deep down want to do. Why not?

Zenquest:

Make a list of things that you've always wanted to do. Now take a look at this list and write down why you shouldn't do each thing. Are those reasons really valid or have you just invented or exaggerated them?

Zenbite:

Life is short, challenge you're reasoning and embrace "Why not?"

CONNECT

Chapter 22: Nature

Nature. It's the source of everything. Connecting with nature has got to be one of the most powerful activities that anyone can do. If there was one thing I could recommend to anyone it's to connect with nature. This connection can come in any form, walking through trees or down the beach, watching the birds in the local park, patting your dog (I think this counts), watching dolphins off the coast, observing ants as they go about their business. There is a power in connecting, observing and experiencing nature. Look around to really observe what is around you in the natural world. Just being in nature (without consciously observing it) can have a benefit on your mind without you even knowing it. There is something relaxing and inspiring about being in nature. The rustle of the trees, the buzz of the bees, the music of the birds, the crash of the waves. Nature has a calming and relaxing soundtrack that can match anything of a classical composer.

Nature in its raw form is independent. Birds don't have a master, grass left untouched will grow and grow, wild horses roam free. It's great to experience nature in a zoo, in the correct zoo where the animals have been rescued and are rehabilitated, not one of those where the animals are dragged from nature and plonked in the middle of a concrete city, but there is a power in seeing nature in its natural setting. It's free and wild. Roaming free and experiencing life to survive and thrive. Make time to experience nature. In the countryside or at the coast it is easy. It's all around us but even in the cities seek out those special places. The places that have been crafted for us to experience. The city parks, the small gardens. They are places to experience nature within all the concrete. They provide a mental sanctuary within all the hustle and bustle. Even without these spaces though, look around, spot the birds, the insects, the mammals living their existence with us. Observing their behaviour can have a relaxing effect on your mind - apart from maybe if the animal is digging around in your rubbish and causing havoc. Aside from some chaos they may cause as they interact with our world, there is a tranquillity in watching nature go about its business. Whether it's animals, insects or plants, there is a relaxing energy and connection with nature that soothes our minds. It relaxes us and makes us feel grateful for the planet that we occupy together with some amazing life.

There are lots of scientific reasons that spending time in nature can help improve your health. Chemicals are released that improve our mind and body (I won't go into these here) but in the end it simply feels good and is relaxing. It's the combination of freedom, wildness, colours, smells and feelings that combine to have a great impact upon our senses. The mountains, canyons, rivers, beaches all created by nature with no intervention from humans. Humans can and do create magnificent things but it's the creations of nature that are the most awe-inspiring and take our breath away. It's self governing and working in harmony with no interaction from us. Nature left to its own devices will not only survive but thrive.

That is probably the most disturbing aspect of humans. The impact that we are having on the planet and therefore the impact on our own minds and bodies. The day that there are no lush green forests or wild animals feeding on the plains is the day we will truly start to die. If all we have is human creation then we are doomed. Nature is wild, raw and the most creative element on the planet. As humans we can think we are superior but nature with all its force through the wind, sun and water can ravage our homes and cities in minutes. We need to respect nature. Respecting nature will allow the planet to thrive and in turn allows us to thrive. We have a symbiotic connection to nature. We are part of nature, we came from nature, we need to maintain our relationship with it to thrive on the planet.

Despite what your belief system is, whether there is a god who created everything or that we came from a single big bang in the cosmos. The single common thread in all these belief systems is that we came from the same thing. In the religious theory, nature and man were created by a single entity and therefore all connected. In the Big Bang theory nature and man were created from a single event and therefore we are all connected. We come from the same stuff. Whichever belief system you follow we are all connected. The same creator or event formed us and the nature that surrounds us. We are all part of the same planet, made from the same chemicals and atoms. That's why connecting to nature is so beneficial to us, we are connected to the raw form of the planet. Spending time in nature is connecting us back to where we came from, we are part of it and we are all connected.

Zenquest:
Go out into nature and observe the sounds and sights. Really take it in, look at the colours, hear the sounds

and feel the ground beneath your feet.

Zenbite:

We are all connected through and to nature.

Chapter 23: See the wonder

One of my favourites, simply see the wonder in the world around you. It's that easy. Look around and see the wonder that is around you in your daily life. From nature, buildings and the people around you. Look in awe at what happens around you on a daily basis, from the small things to the big things that are around us all the time, some may be right in front of us others may be on the broader world stage. Ants building a nest, birds flying across the sky, nature puts on a free show. See the detail and attention in buildings old and new (maybe not those 1970s grey monstrosities), see the care that the architects took in designing the building, the small details that you don't register. Ever noticed the carvings and monuments such as eagles or gargoyles placed upon the top of buildings. Next time you're in a city take a look up and observe the detail that is there every day for us to see. Look at the city parks full of life right there in the city, from nature to the hustle and bustle of the people living there. We just need to look. Look down to see what is around our feet, look up to see what is in the sky. Take a look at the clouds and all their incredible formations, like works of art on nature's wall.

See wonder in the chaos that lies within our cities. Wonder at how it all comes together in a 24/7 ongoing circle. All the small things combine together to allow our towns and cities to operate, mostly, in harmony. Even the traffic can be a wonder, where are all these people going, what are they doing with their days? They all have lives that they are living, getting to places to see people. See the wonder in how we all live and work together. Sure there are conflicts but see the wonder in people coming together to solve problems. See the positive in the negative, the annoying fly that keeps zooming past your face, where is that fly going, where did it come from, how does it fly so fast? There is wonder all around us and it doesn't need to be the big things, the little things, the small details can contain just as much wonder.

The key is to observe, you don't need to look for it as it's right there in front of us as part of our everyday lives. Grabbing your morning coffee, just that simple task. Let's break it down. First it requires the beans to be planted by a farmer, who started the farm to provide for his family, the beans are then picked by workers, then packed and sold to market in their raw form, then they are purchased by another who transforms the beans into a product to be sold. That product requires someone to get the beans into a bag, transported around the world, marketed to business so that they purchase them. Then once they have made their way around the world, they enter the final straight, into the hands of a barista who learnt they trade to create the perfect coffee having woken up at 4am that morning to travel to work to meet the morning rush. The barista works in a coffee shop that is run by the small business owner, a couple who have 3 children, they have a dream to be free and run their own business, they fund, market and operate the coffee shop day to day, purchasing products, hiring staff, advertising their business within the town of city. The shop has been fitted out so you can queue in a nice environment, all the furniture had to be made and purchased, to the machine that takes your payment via your mobile phone, using technology developed by people all around the world working together to create a complete payment system which just requires a touch of your phone. Let's not get started on how the mobile phone is designed, built, shipped and marketed all over the world. Finally after all these steps, processes and people you have your morning coffee. That for me is a wonder. All those moving parts coming together to allow such a simple, yet so complex task and set of events.

See the wonder in the world, it's a compelling, challenging, quiet, noisy, beautiful, amazing place that is on your doorstep every day. Observing this everyday life makes you appreciate everything you have in your life. The friends and family that support you, even if they drive you mad sometimes. The sunrise that brings a new day, and the sunset to mark the close of another day to begin the night. It's amazing to just look around and experience the world and all it has to offer. It may make you feel big, it may make you feel small, it may make you feel connected and maybe disconnected. It's an amazing world, see it, smell it, listen to it, use all your senses to experience it. You just need to look for the wonder that is around us. We are all busy, or we all appear to be busy, or we feel busy, but take time to enjoy the simple wonders around you. You don't need to travel halfway around the world to see wonder and amazement, it's all there in front of you. Sure take the trip, I'm the first to jump on a plane and see the world, just don't forget the wonder that is there every day in your daily routine. Don't forget the people in your life that bring you joy every day, simply just by being there.

Take it all in, it's easy to forget and take it for granted but it's there to be enjoyed and appreciated. We just need to remember to look.

Once you start to appreciate the wonder that is in the world and around you, you will start to feel gratitude for your life and your time on this planet. Connecting to nature and people, seeing the wonder that is there it will relax your mind and body. It will make you appreciate the small things in life, it will make you appreciate the big things in life. Just take the time.

Zenquest:

Take a walk and simply look around at all the amazing things happening around you. Did you notice these things before?

Zenbite:

Stop and see the wonder in the world.

Chapter 24: Music

All the physical senses of sight, sound and smell can provide amazing experiences and ways to express ourselves. They provide understanding and awareness of the world around us. They can change your mood from one minute to the next and change your understanding and appreciation of an experience. Think of a sound or smell that has transported you back to your childhood, a memorable place or time. For me cinnamon makes it feel like Christmas which transports me back to my childhood and the fun family times I had at that time of year. The senses provide a portal into the world and also our soul, they pick up minor changes in our environment which evokes emotions and responses in us. Some we can understand, others we haven't got the foggiest why we feel that way (foggiest is a UK slang reference to not having an idea). They are powerful throughout our lives and they change our experience of the world. All the senses provide this power, for me though the power of sound and the power of music astounds me everyday. This may not apply to everyone but for me there is something special about the collection of notes, sounds and voices that have been crafted and combined together by another human being, creating art that can transform you to a different time, place or mood. It's something you can't see, it's in the airwaves, travelling as far as it can reach. We can't see it and that makes it even more special and mysterious.

Often the occasions within our life, whether they be positive or negative can have a soundtrack alongside them. When we have a party, the music is an integral part, it sets the mood and tone of the night. It determines the mood of those at the party. There is a completely different vibe listening to the rock of AC/DC to the calm of Jack Johnson. It can change the mood of a party, gathering and experience. Music can make us feel sad, taking us back to a previous incident or remembering someone who is no longer with us. Our memories can be bitter and sweet all at the same time and music can take us there. At the same time it can uplift us and remind us of the good times, taking us back to a happy time that fills us with joy. We get that smile on our face that we just can't explain and we feel great. Even if there is no attachment to a particular song, just listening to music can create an emotion in us that fills the whole of our bodies and minds. Listening to music provides the soundtrack to our lives. It can help us through good and bad times. It's there with us on the journey. There is something special about another human being creating a sound that connects deep with us, bringing us joy or sadness, making us dance or take a seat to contemplate life. It brings us together in joy and sadness. We have to admire the artist who created the music, expressing themselves, being vulnerable to show their emotions to the world and also showing their creation to the world. It requires a level of skill to combine voice and musical talents to create a sound that will stop others in their tracks.

Importantly it's not just the music it's the words. Sometimes the words make sense and have deep meaning, other times it's just the beat and pattern of the words that just work and resonate with us. The beat of the music and the words combine to create a unique sound and experience. Connect with music, listen to the words and feel the beat. It can get us to move our bodies in joy and the next minute bring us to our knees in sadness. Bring music into your life, let it be the soundtrack of your life. It provides an emotional backdrop to our experiences. A life without music is a life without rhythm or emotion. Let the music enter your body and mind. Let it wash over you and take your experiences to the next level. Music resonates through your body through vibrations, the vibrating airwaves hitting your ear drums but also the skin on your body, the hairs on your arms picking up the sounds in the airwaves that can transform your whole body. Let the music into your body, let it flow from your soul into your mind and body. The key is to feel the music, without feeling music is just noise, with feeling the sound is transformed into music and that's the key. The transformation of sound from just noise into music through the collection and integration of the beat, voice and instruments but also how you the receiver interprets the sounds. For some, dance music is just noise, they don't feel it. As the receiver the sounds don't resonate with them, however for others dance music will lift their soul and it will take them to new higher places. This applies to any genre of music, not just dance. Find the music that resonates with you and transforms it from just sounds to music that makes you feel alive.

There is something about music and the connection to the body, some not all music makes you want to move. Whether it's a full blown break dance or a simple nod of the head. Either way your body wants to move when it hears the beat. Let the music allow your body to move. To do this you often have to get your mind out of the way. Your ego may be embarrassed, I can't dance, I don't want to dance in front of others. It's a great example of when we can stop ourselves from doing something that we want to do but our mind, taking in the situation and circumstances will stop our bodies from moving and going with the music For many, their experience of listening to music in private can be very different to how they experience it in public. For some they will rave along in the privacy of their own room, only to resort to a head bob once out in public. On the flip side, others will feel the rhythm and presence of others and the room to take their dancing to the next level. The experience will become communal, they will feed off the energy of others to take their experience to the next level. The key is to go with what is comfortable for you in that time and place. Just feel the music.

Zenquest:
Put on your favourite song or artist, listen to the music, feel the rhythm, the beat and the words. Give yourself time to really enjoy music and the feelings it brings. Move your body to really feel the music. How does it make you feel?

Zenbite:
Connect and feel music to add a soundtrack to your life.

Chapter 25: Time

Time is the one thing we cannot control. It is always marching forward and we can never get it back, until Doc Brown finally cracks the flux capacitor (Back to the Future movie reference for those who have no idea what I'm talking about) we are servants to time. It moves forward without any control from us. We all have a limited amount of time on this planet and we can't change that. What we can change is our perception and appreciation of time. We can't change the pace at which time moves forward but we can change how we perceive it. Ever had two minutes to get ready and be out of the door, how quick does that two minutes disappear. On the flip side, when you have a two minute timer running on your electric toothbrush, how long does that two minutes last? It's like an eternity, quite often I never make the full two minutes and bail out before it's finished. Two minutes, that's all it is but it seems like a lifetime. On both occasions the time is only two minutes but the experience and the velocity that time appears to move forward is vastly different. If you watch time hoping it will move forward fast, the world seems to stand still. If you ignore time and just go with the flow, it just seems to disappear. The difference is our perception of time and our ability to bend time so that it slows down. The thing is, we can alter our perception of time to give ourselves time back. I know that sounds crazy but it's possible. If you observe time and respect it you can slow time down. Don't waste it. Time is precious, you'll never get it back.

A few years ago I quit the rat race and one thing I noticed was that whilst in work I was wishing the time away. Wishing for 5pm so I could finish, wishing for Friday afternoon so I could finish for the weekend, wishing away the weeks so that I could go on that family holiday in 4 weeks. I was constantly wishing time away, wishing it would fast forward so that I could get out of work and do something more interesting. Wishing away time is not good. Time is valuable. Time with family, time with friends, time to do what you want. Hold your time close, it's yours, use it wisely and don't waste it away. Don't do things that make you wish time away, in the end it's not worth it. Once I quit the rat race I appreciated time much more. I was no longer wishing the days away. I was actually wanting time to slow down so I had more time in my day to enjoy it.

More time in the week and more time at the weekend. I valued my time to do as much as possible in the time I had available. I started to notice things a lot more. I went from wishing the day would get to 5pm to wanting it to slow down so I could get in as much as I could. The clock would get to 14:40, school pick up time before I knew it, and this is when I noticed that previously I had been wishing the day away. Now I wanted time to go as slow as possible. This then spread to the whole week, to the whole month. I wanted time to travel as slow as possible so I could enjoy it and savour it. I started to value my time a lot more. No longer was I wishing the time away. I started to appreciate the time I had. It started to spread to other areas, time with the kids, time spent with family, time spent with friends. Just to enjoy it all and soak it all up. I looked for more enjoyment from my time. I recognised its value and all the times I had wished time away. I had wished away the one thing I could never get back. Use your time wisely, spend it doing what you love, spend it with those you love. Take time for yourself. Slow down and enjoy the time you have with others and on your own. It's all valuable. Appreciating time will increase your fulfilment from life, you will achieve more things than you thought possible and importantly spend time doing the things you love.

Kids grow up fast, older members of the family grow old fast and before you know it your life around you and the people in it are changing. Don't fear time, it's inevitable. People and things get old, it's part of life. It's part of the journey. Just learn to appreciate it. Once you start to appreciate, just in the same way as appreciating nature and people around you, your life will begin to shift. You will get more fulfilment, you will see the positivity in life and not the negative. You will be more grateful for those people and things in your life, as you know your time with them could be limited, and in doing so your joy will increase. Value you time and you will give yourself the gift of enjoying life and slowing time down to appreciate it even more. In the modern world it's easy to rush from one thing to the next, to get to the next place, to do the next thing. See the destination, look where you are going next but appreciate the journey, appreciate the time it takes to get to the destination. Got a 5 hour journey on the train or car? Look around, enjoy the scenery, listen to some of your favourite music, and connect with your passengers. It's not a 5 hour long and draining car journey, it's 5 hours to connect with people and things that you love. It's 5 hours of your time that you could spend on your own, 5 hours you could spend listening to an audio book. 5 hours of time in which you can appreciate life. It might not seem like that but you can reframe pretty much everything in life. Time is one of them, reframe how you see an activity and you will reframe your experience of that time. Turn a negative into a positive. Reframe how you see those meaningless tasks to something more positive. How can you reframe the time spent doing an activity to something positive. Question yourself, do I need to even do this activity, is it worth my time? Am I just doing it because I feel like I have to or I actually need or want to do it? Once you value your time, you will start to prioritise the things that are important to you, once you begin to do this you will increase your fulfilment of your time and life.

Zenquest:
Take a look at your week, how do you spend your time? Are you spending it how you would like? Change your daily routine to appreciate and enjoy your time. Start to reframe everyday tasks and begin to appreciate them more.

Zenbite:
Take the time to enjoy life doing the things you love.

Chapter 26: People

Take time out of your day to connect to others, whether you're an introvert or an extrovert, connecting to others can transform your day. If you connect with others in a positive way it can enhance your mood, bring a smile to your face and make you feel part of the world around you. Connecting to someone is a fundamental behaviour. We are social beings, without connection to others we can feel low, lost and lonely. Even if that connection is only brief, take advantage of it, seek it out. Sometimes you're busy in your day, you don't feel like you have time to connect, you see someone across the corridor or on the street and think "I don't want to talk, I don't have the time, I'm too busy", it can be easy to shrug the connection aside but take it, unless the other person is your sworn enemy, someone that drives you crazy, or rubs you up the wrong way, a simple interaction with another person can really enhance your mood and could potentially transform your day. It's a chance to start a deep conversation, learn something new or simply just to connect. Some find it easy to talk and connect with others, some find it hard. Either way the connection to someone can benefit your soul. It doesn't have to be a deep and meaningful conversion, sometimes it's valuable to get things off your mind, to share the load and get another's perspective. Sometimes though, these conversations can feel hard, either we don't want to share our deep feelings, we don't have the energy or simply we aren't in the mood. I say that's fine, we don't always have to maintain deep conversations and connections with everyone, sometimes a simple chat is enough to connect to someone. Don't get me wrong, even though sometimes it's hard, if every single interaction was a surface level conversation then we wouldn't get the level of connection that is required. On the flip side constant and continuous deep connection can be tiring and emotionally draining. Keep the balance, connect with others on a deeper level (as deep as you can) and also maintain the chit chat conversations. It will provide balance to your interactions with others. Surface level connections and conversations can sometimes be dismissed as not valuable, but they are. They allow us to have a connection with someone on a level that's easy, not every conversation has to be war and peace and a discussion about your deepest secrets. Sometimes we just need that connection with someone else to learn about their day but importantly for others to ask about us. Yes, we want to know about others, what they are doing or thinking but really deep down we also want others to ask about us. Ever had a conversation with someone and they just talk about themselves, whether it's surface level or deep, either way the conversation can eventually get boring. This person just wants to hear their own voice, they just want to hear their own opinions. Like most things in life, it's about balance. Enquire about others, ask them how they are, delve deeper if it's appropriate but also allow others to ask about you. This may sound self centred but it's not, you deserve to discuss your own thoughts and opinions. A conversation that is one way is not a conversation, it's a speech and a statement from one person to another. It's not a two way transaction. Be kind to others, listen, learn but invite others to learn about you and allow you to share your feelings and thoughts.

As we interact with others we can come across those that are negative or positive. People aren't necessarily one extreme or the other, but you will come across those that are generally more negative (glass half empty) and those that are more positive (glass half full). Throughout our lives we will need different types of people in our lives. Sometimes, yes we need to hear the hard truths, not everything is great, some things are negative. Listen to those negative opinions, but use them to learn and grow. They can be turned into a positive to learn something new and grow. Take the negative interaction or view point and turn it into a positive. Don't dismiss those in your life that have a tendency to be negative, but also don't surround yourself with them. If you surround yourself with negative people then life will feel hard and painful. The world will seem dark and dull. You need positive people in your life, those that bring light to the day, they bring life to the party, they look at the positive in life. It can also be said don't surround yourself with only positive people, they will just tell you good news, but I would personally prefer to be surrounded by positive not negative people all day. Respect those that have a negative tendency, give them time but don't get dragged down by them. They may have valuable insights for you to expand and learn but look to the positive. You know those in your life that have a negative view and those that have a positive view. Welcome and embrace those with a positive attitude into your life. They will drive you forward and encourage you to improve yourself, they will encourage you to try new things, they will encourage you to embrace life. They will see the positive in the negative and help you turn the dark into the light. Be one of those people yourself. If you think positively, then positive things will flow to you. Think negatively and negative things will flow to you. Be the light not in just your life but in the life of others. You don't have to go around high fiving everyone like someone out of an American 'bro' movie. You just need to look at the positive and send this out in your interactions with others. In this way you will draw positive people towards you and in turn positive things will start to happen. You could brighten someone's day with your positivity. If you know people who are generally negative you can also start to guide them towards positivity. This could be harder than it sounds but sometimes people need to see the positive light and have a positive connection in their day. It's an opportunity to enhance someone's day, check in how they are, enquire about them, show interest, connect to them, and provide positive support to their situation. Even just being an ear to someone can enhance their day, it will allow them to get things off their chest. It could turn their negative day into a positive. The start to it all is to connect. Once you connect with others this opens the door to change, growth and learning.

Whilst connecting to others is valuable, I mean it's a core part of life, connecting to yourself is as important, if not more. What does that mean though, connecting to yourself? To some it will feel natural and instinctive but to others it may sound weird. To me, connecting to yourself is to connect to the inner you. That person inside who doesn't always get to come out, who doesn't always get heard or who doesn't always get to shine. It's the real you, the you where your emotions and feelings live, the you where your aspirations live, the you where your views and opinions live. The real you doesn't always come out to others, and that's fine, we don't always want to show our true selves to others, especially those that we don't feel connected to or comfortable around. We should feel connected to ourselves though, get to know yourself, what are your dreams, goals, what are your opinions on topics. I know it may sound strange but not everyone is connected to themselves and who they really are. We've stacked up a bunch of layers and masks on top of our real selves. We've taken what others think about others and made it our own view of ourselves. We've taken on other people's behaviours and made them our own and now we believe that is what we are all about. We've put ourselves in a box that we've either given to ourselves or others have given to us. Sounds like a mess right? It's just part of life as we grow, learn and develop ourselves. We don't always do the things that are true to ourselves. We may take a job that we think we should take, we may buy a house that we should move into, we may date someone that we should love, we may be friends with some because we think they are similar to us and we should have a connection. We do all these things whether consciously or unconsciously, moulding our world around others without being true to ourselves. It's easy to do, we do it to fit it, to not upset others, to be part of the team or family. We do it to feel part of the group or clan and to feel valued. So if you're reading this, don't beat yourself up, it happens to all of us. We get caught up in the race and the noise of the world and we forget who we truly are. How do we 'fix' it? We connect to ourselves, we become our new best friend, we take ourselves out for a date or day trip. We look after ourselves, we take time to listen to ourselves, we let our voice speak and importantly be heard not only by others, but by ourselves. We actually listen to our own intuition and inner voice, what do I want to do? What do I want from this situation? It doesn't mean we ignore or disregard others, it means we listen to our own inner voice, we connect to the person that is inside that may have got buried or lost along the way of life. Connect to that person. Take time out of your day to really think about how you feel about a situation, person or topic. What do you feel? What do you want to do? What is your opinion? Take time out for yourself, it's the best thing that you can do to connect. A simple task is to go for a walk, just on your own, listen to your thoughts, respect your thoughts, hear them and process them. Give them the respect and time you would want others to give to you. Give yourself respect first. Once you start to value and respect yourself then others will do this too. Connect to the inner you.

Zenquest:
How often do you connect with others? Do you embrace those opportunities or do you shy away? If you shy away, next time an opportunity arises to connect with someone, take it!

Take time to go for a walk on your own, listen to your thoughts, I mean really listen to them. What are they telling you?

Zenbite:
Connection is a core human behaviour. Connect to

others, connect to yourself. Embrace it.

Chapter 27: Confidence

Confidence can be a strange thing, being too confident can get you into trouble. As a kid too much confidence riding your bike down a 20ft slope with no practice but a bunch of confidence, could see you in a great big heap or it could see you as the champion of the bike trail with your friends, held aloft on their shoulders "did you see what he did and that summersault at the end, wow." Too much confidence can see you pushing people away, whilst others will thrive and be driven towards this confident person in the middle of the room, others will shy away. Even those that are driven towards a person with lots of confidence can be put off "she's wayyy over the top, even too much for me." Too little confidence can be just as powerful, but for the opposite reasons. Too little confidence can see you being overlooked for a job promotion "they're a great person and a hard worker but I just don't see the confidence to take it to the next level". Too little confidence can create a nervousness in those around you, you're not confident so you give off a non-confident vibe. Giving off that nervous energy can unsettle others, you don't know it's happening and neither do they but they know something is off. Too little confidence can hinder you and hold you back, it can endear you to some but in the wide world too little confidence can be like having a handicap. On the flip side, jumping in and being too confident can drive others away, the energy is too much, they get a bad vibe, others can feel the sparks flying off you. You can be just too much for other people to handle.

As always in life, the key is balance. Walking down a mountain slope, too little confidence will see you slipping on the way down, you're not sure footed enough and before you know it you're on your arse sliding down trying to avoid the big rocks when things could get even more sketchy. Too much confidence will pretty much result in the same outcome, you bound down at a fast pace, don't quite judge your footing as you are too confident, you misstep and find yourself in the same situation as the nervous guy who was slowly making their way down the mountain. Walk down, take your time, be sure footed, put your feet down with a solid action, keep moving but observe what is around you, respect the mountain. This is the same in life, be bold, be solid in your steps forward, have conviction in your views but be respectful of those around you and your surroundings, don't rush decisions unless they feel right, be confident in your actions. Overly confident will backfire like a slap in the face when you thought you were on top of the world and you were the best. It will bring you down, you went too hard, too fast. Life will correct you and set you back into your place. That doesn't mean shy away and hide, too little confidence will set you back in life. You will question yourself too much, you won't listen to your intuition as your non-confident ego will get in the way. Stopping you from moving forward, keeping you in the same spot when you know you should and could move forward. Respect yourself with confidence in yourself, move forward, be kind, be balanced in your approach. Not overly confident but not under confident. Quite often I use the example of two people who have the same skill level going for a new job, they are both equally matched in their skillset with a similar background, both would be great at the job. However, one is quietly confident whilst the other is shy and quiet, I'm pretty sure in 90% of cases it will be the candidate who shows solid confidence that will get the job. They show a quality that shows they are strong and will be able to adapt to what is put in front of them. The quiet candidate doesn't give off the same vibe, when things are getting hard will this person step up? This doesn't mean those that are shy can't thrive, I just mean that if you are confident in yourself it will show to others. Show that you have confidence in yourself. If you can't show confidence in yourself, why should someone else? It doesn't mean everyone has to go around being super confident all of the time, that would be annoying and result in over confidence and lots of annoying people. Be confident in yourself and your abilities, be measured, be calm, show that you know your stuff to others whilst also respecting their opinions and space.

I also believe that confidence can come in different forms. I call them 'inner confidence' and 'outer confidence'. Outer confidence is the confidence you show to the outside world and how you appear to others. With high outer confidence, you show a confident appearance and outlook to those around you, you make confident decisions and step forward with confidence. Low outer confidence looks a little different, you're a bit more shy around others, your decisions involve others a lot more, you question yourself in group situations, you may not put your opinions forward. Neither high or low outer confidence is a bad thing, they're just different. Then there is your inner confidence, this is the confidence that is deep down in your core, your core beliefs and views that you have in yourself. High inner confidence allows you to step forward and deal with life's challenges, nothing phases you, you have a strong inner confidence that comes from deep down, you know you can do it, you take the big challenges in life without questioning yourself too much, you have confidence in yourself. With low inner confidence, your core confidence isn't so sure footed, you take more time to make decisions, you question yourself more, you don't have that deep down confidence in yourself. Now for the interesting part, I believe that people can have a mix, just because your inner confidence is high doesn't mean your outer confidence is high and vice versa.

You may have low inner confidence and low outer confidence, this means you question yourself a lot, you aren't confident in your own decisions, in group settings you don't voice your opinions in case you get shot down, you follow with the group rather than lead, you shy away from others. You will question your own decisions in private and question your place within the group. You can feel overwhelmed by all sorts of scenarios that make you withdraw into yourself. Those in the situation are best talking to someone to start taking steps to improve their situation and start to gain confidence. Start simple, start small but take those steps.

Low inner confidence with high outer confidence allows you to be more confident when with others, inside you are nervous and your stomach is churning at a 100 miles an hour but you are able to confidently make group decisions, appearing confident to friends and colleagues. Once you get out of a group situation you may feel relieved, you did well but you are glad to be out of the situation. Take steps to build your inner confidence by seeing all the good things you have within your life and the decisions you have made in the past, don't dismiss small decisions and achievements as insignificant.

High inner confidence with low outer confidence is an interesting one, within a group setting you may stay out of the limelight, you contribute to the team but you don't put your neck on the line. You are confident within yourself and your abilities but within a group or social setting some of your confidence is lost. You can feel conflicted at times, you have an idea to put forward that you just know will work but you question yourself and withdraw in the setting. On your own though, in your own decisions you thrive as you aren't influenced by the group setting. Take time to build your confidence, start small by putting yourself out there. Don't go jumping in with both feet, but use your inner confidence to feed your outer confidence. You know deep down you've got this.

High inner and outer confidence is where you are confident within yourself across all kinds of scenarios and situations. You are confident in your own decisions whether you are making them for yourself or others. You are happy to voice your opinions to others and have an inner strength to do so. You may be a leader within a group or business, you put ideas forward and are confident to lead and be adventurous. Be humble and appreciate those around you, help others to gain their own confidence.

Throughout our life I believe we will shift between phases of confidence as we age and move through different phases of life. As we become parents, bosses, grandparents, leaders, team leaders our confidence will shift. For example you could be highly confident inside and out but then you start a new job which sets your confidence back. This can be seen in school children moving from primary to high school, in primary school they are the top dogs but once they get to high school they are back to the bottom, so to speak. We could also have a different mix of confidence depending upon the situation. At home we could be highly confident in ourselves with our family and friends, we are the leader of the pack but at work we withdraw within that environment and our confidence is much lower. The situation and the environment can influence our confidence even across our day. Life changes and we will change with it, our confidence in ourselves and our interaction with the world around us will ebb and flow.

Confidence in the correct balance can be a powerful thing. It will endear you to people. Those that are overly confident will themselves a little in you, they will recognise the confidence that you show. Those who don't have the confidence will see you as someone they can look up to and aspire to be. The key is having confidence in yourself and your abilities, you are unique in your skills and attributes. Allow your inner and outer confidence to develop, be kind to yourself there is no one else like you on the planet, you offer something no other human being can offer, a combination that is unique to you. Show confidence in yourself.

Zenquest:

Think of a time when you haven't been confident, what was the outcome? Would the outcome have been different if you had shown a little more confidence?

How would you rate your inner and outer confidence?

Zenbite:

Be confident in yourself, you are unique, but be balanced and respectful.

BRINGING IT ALL TOGETHER

Chapter 28: Happiness

As we draw to a close and reflect, I hope this book has given you some learnings to take away and incorporate into your daily life. The key to real happiness is to understand and accept that ultimately we are all individually responsible for our own happiness. Yes others can influence and affect our days and life but it's down to you how you handle and frame that interaction. You can't rely on others to make you happy, it has to come from within. Bad things will and do happen, it's how you handle the bad things that determines your happiness. Do you let it consume you and move into wallowing and self pity or do you process the event, accept the situation, forgive the other person and move towards happiness. Quite often we can point to others and events that have happened to us "she did this, he did that, this happened, that happened." Sure these things do happen but you shouldn't let others rule your happiness, you are responsible for your happiness and how you approach your day. For some this may seem logical, for others it may sound totally wrong. Everyone is open to their own opinion, that's the beauty in life, but to have a life where your happiness is framed and controlled by others and not you is not a true path to being happy and enjoying life. It's actually a great thing to know that you are in control of your happiness and not someone else. You determine your own destiny. Others can support you, guide you and help you on your way. They will be there when the times are tough, sometimes they won't be there when the times are tough. You don't have to go through life just relying on yourself, that no one can help and that it's just down to you. Others can guide and support you but once you accept that your happiness is generated from within then you can lead a more fulfilled and happy life. You control your mind and how it frames things, you control how you handle the stress within your mind and body, your intuition comes from within not outside. You can learn to appreciate what you have in your life, treat others with respect and observe and appreciate the little things in life. When things go wrong you are in control of what you take away from that experience, do you see it as a negative or a chance to grow and learn. People can help you find your purpose, but it's down to you to find a purpose that is right for you, your purpose is for you and not another person. Your purpose may help others but it's your choice to help others. See the fun in life to allow the happiness to come in, spend the time with people you love and do things that bring you fun. The actions that you take, not someone else's, define you. Finding the power of no is to be true to yourself and protect and preserve your boundaries. Embrace your experiences in life, to learn and grow and create happiness in your days. How you embrace and connect with the world around you through nature and music will bring you happiness, find your own connection to the world around you. Connect with what brings a smile to your face. Be confident in yourself to be the person who you are. If you lead a life that is true to you then you can truly be happy, just remember that you determine your happiness not someone else.

Chapter 29: That's a wrap

For me sometimes when I get to the end of a book I'm like that was great but I just can't remember all of the key points. So here we go, here is your Barely Zen summary. The bit you can skip to for a quick read to jog your memory. This book was never about perfection or rigid rules, it's about offering tools and insights to help you live with more balance, awareness, and authenticity. Life, after all, is a work in progress—a series of small moments that collectively shape who we are.

The Power of Awareness

Whether it's recognising the hidden stressors in your life, listening to your intuition, or simply pausing to breathe, awareness is the first step towards meaningful change. By noticing what's happening in your mind and body, you can start to make choices that align with your values and well-being.

Mindfulness in Action

Mindfulness isn't just about meditation or quiet moments; it's about showing up fully in your life. It's about appreciating the little things—a warm cup of tea, the laughter of your children, or the feeling of the sun on your face. When you make space to savour these moments, you create a foundation of gratitude and presence that can sustain you even during challenging times.

Balance and Flow

Finding balance isn't about achieving a perfect 50/50 split in every area of your life. Instead, it's about tuning into what feels right for you. Balance might mean allowing yourself to indulge in something small that brings you joy or saying no to commitments that drain your energy. Flow, on the other hand, is about trusting yourself and the natural rhythm of life. When you let go of overthinking and follow your intuition, life tends to unfold in surprising and beautiful ways.

The Mind-Body Connection

Your thoughts, emotions, and physical health are deeply interconnected. By caring for your body—through movement, rest, and nourishment—you also care for your mind. And by managing mental stress, you can reduce its impact on your physical well-being. Together, these practices create a powerful feedback loop of vitality and resilience.

Compassion and Forgiveness

As you move forward, remember to treat yourself and others with compassion. Forgiveness is not about excusing harm but about freeing yourself from the weight of resentment. Similarly, extending kindness to others—even in small, everyday ways—can ripple out and create positive change beyond what you might imagine.

Your Journey Ahead

The beauty of life lies in its imperfection and unpredictability. You won't always get it right, and that's okay. This book isn't a roadmap with a set destination; it's a toolkit to help you navigate your unique path. Use what resonates, adapt what feels right, and leave behind what doesn't. Trust that even small steps can lead to significant transformation over time.

As you close this book, my hope is that you feel inspired to embrace life's messiness, cherish its beauty, and keep growing into the best version of yourself. Remember, you are your greatest guide. Trust your intuition, savour the moments, and let life flow. Thank you for joining me on this journey. Now, go out and create your version of zen.

That's a wrap

You've made it this far, or you just jumped to the end of the book (fair play), if you like artwork inspired by landscapes and nature please visit stemarsh.com for art captured by yours truly.

About the Author

Steve Marsh is a writer, photographer, and accidental philosopher whose work blends dry wit with quiet observation. Born in Wigan, a working-class town in the north of England, Steve grew up with a healthy dose of northern humour and a knack for finding meaning in the mundane. In his twenties, he packed his bags and moved to Australia in search of something more—sunshine, freedom, perspective… and maybe a slightly slower pace of life.

That leap became a turning point. Surrounded by Australia's wide open spaces and salt-soaked coastlines, Steve found the space to reflect, create, and explore what it means to live a life that's both thoughtful and lighthearted. Whether behind the lens or in front of the keyboard, his work encourages people to pause, notice the small things, and approach life with curiosity, humour, and a bit more care.

Steve's work is a refreshingly honest and often funny take on navigating the chaos of modern living with a little less stress and a little more perspective. Through a mix of humour, reflection, and everyday insight, he encourages readers to slow down, laugh at themselves, and maybe—even just a little—rethink how they show up in the world.

When he's not writing or shooting photographs, you'll find him exploring the Australian coastline, indulging in long walks and runs, tinkering with technology or answering an endless stream of wonderfully weird questions from his kids.